Memory Fitness
Over 40

1996 Dear Maria:
Best Wishes on
remembering your
40TH Birthday...
or what is it?...
40 I Q; 40TH Percentile;
40 M.P.H. Let me
Know if you
remember!
Love,
Bart

1996 Dear Marie:

Memory Fitness
Over 40

BY ROBIN WEST, PH.D.

Triad Publishing Company / Gainesville, Florida

Printed in the United States of America

Library of Congress Cataloging in Publication Data

West, Robin, 1951–
    Memory fitness over 40.

    Bibliography: p.
    Includes index.
    1. Memory—Age factors.   2. Mnemonics.   I. Title.
II. Title: Memory fitness over forty. [DNLM: 1. Aging—
popular works.   2. Memory—popular works.   BF 371 W519m]
BF378.A33W46 1985   153.1′2   85-16496
ISBN 0-937404-21-7

To my family

Contents

Foreword

Anyone who has worked with adults of varying ages recognizes the need for a book like *Memory Fitness Over 40*. Whenever middle-aged and older adults come into laboratories to participate in research, concerns about "failing" memory are quickly revealed by the questions they ask and the anxiety they express. To support these impressions, scientific surveys reveal that loss of memory ability is one of the most common fears about growing older. Although there are numerous memory improvement books available, none so clearly addresses itself to the unique memory problems of the later years.

This book is long overdue and Dr. Robin West is very well suited to write it. She first entered our laboratory at Washington University 10 years ago as an enterprising college graduate looking for employment in psychology. Since then, she has acquired considerable research expertise in gerontology, and has provided advice on memory improvement to countless individuals. With the right mix of academic and practical experience, she can convey laboratory findings in a way that shows their relationship to real-world memory concerns.

Memory Fitness Over 40 fulfills two very important functions: 1) to present accurate information for the lay person about memory and aging, and 2) to provide sensible recommendations for everyday memory improvement that can be used by people of all ages. The first half of the book concentrates on explaining how memory works and its relationship to aging, including the influence of health and self-concept. It examines Alzheimer's disease and suggests ways to distinguish normal memory problems from dementia, and ways to overcome stereotyped fears about growing old. The second half of the book fulfills the other function, providing recommendations for improving attention and concentration, remembering new information, and recalling things from the past. Special chapters focus on remembering names and faces, and medications.

At a time when Alzheimer's disease and the debilitation of aging are receiving enormous publicity, *Memory Fitness Over 40* represents a welcome change. Although there is a relationship between age-related changes in the brain and memory decline, the inevitability and irreversibility of this decline is not yet established. Gerontologists have considerable evidence that older adults' skills can be improved on both memory and intelligence tests. For this reason, Dr. West takes an upbeat approach. The age-related memory changes that are described are not viewed as irreversible. Instead, she focuses on ways to achieve memory success in daily life through interventions in the areas of health, self-concept, environment, and memory strategy usage.

This book treats memory in all its complexity. It points out that illness and medications can reduce memory ability temporarily, that anxiety about memory plays a critical role in determining one's success as a memorizer, and that attentiveness to one's surroundings is essential to prevent memory errors. The book does an excellent job of describing the memory skill of the older person not as a one-dimensional entity but as a reflection of the interaction of many factors.

Memory Fitness Over 40 is recommended for anyone concerned with memory and aging because it is clearly written and based on extant research. Although the memory improvement recommendations emphasize methods for persons experiencing normal memory problems, the information contained in the book may be useful for those with more serious memory disabilities. This book should be valuable reading for middle-aged and older adults; social workers, nurses and other professionals working with them; and finally, for concerned family members.

Department of Psychology   JACK BOTWINICK, PHD
Aging and Development Program
Washington University
St. Louis, Missouri

Acknowledgments

This book is dedicated to my family because they never asked me to settle for less. My parents, Donna, and Ken encouraged and unfailingly supported every endeavor I chose to undertake. The enthusiasm and confidence in me expressed by all of my family, including my in-laws, has meant a great deal to me. Special thanks to Ken for serving as a foil for my ideas, for letting me monopolize our computer, and for gently nudging me back to life whenever I started to get obsessive about the book. My children, Dara and Jaina, deserve big hugs and kisses for being very well-behaved. Along with Ken, they provided a fun escape from the work.

Heartfelt appreciation is extended to Susan Norton, for providing patient and loving care for Jaina.

I would like to thank my mentors, including Dick Odom, who

taught me academic writing, and Keith Clayton, who introduced me to the complexity and excitement of memory research. More than anyone else, I am indebted to Martha Storandt and Jack Botwinick, who first sparked my interest in cognition and aging. Over the last 10 years they have been constant advisors, sounding boards, and cheerleaders. I admire them very much, both for their accomplishments as academicians, and for their willingness to be steady guides for young scholars like myself.

I appreciate the assistance of Bob Schleser, Lynn Boatwright, and Dave Harrison, who assisted me in the development of some of these ideas. Thanks also go to Mary Whisenant and Cecile Chapman, who helped with the typing.

At Triad Publishing Company, Becky Howard and Lorna Rubin worked tirelessly to edit this manuscript. They took someone trained in academic writing and dragged her (kicking and screaming!) into the mass market. They deserve much of the credit for any success this book achieves.

University of Florida
Gainesville, Florida

ROBIN L. WEST

Introduction

Many of us have unrealistically low expectations of our abilities as we get older. One of the factors that erodes our confidence and prevents us from realizing our full potential is the fear that something is happening to our memory.

We may see little signs—forgetting a lunch date, mislaying our keys, beginning a sentence and suddenly forgetting what we were about to say, starting to introduce someone we know and finding that our memory for the name is a complete blank. It's easy to believe the worst—our memory is going.

All of us are regularly exposed to the stereotype of the forgetful older person. Because we've heard so much about Alzheimer's disease—especially if a relative suffers with it—we fear that anything we forget is a sign that we will be next. These stereotypes and fears lead us to devalue our abilities, and, subsequently, act in ways that further reduce memory skill. While I was writing this book, almost everyone I told about it reacted by saying, "I need that! Let me know as soon as it's finished."

This book offers a realistic appraisal of what to expect from your memory as you get older. Much of the information is based on psychological research into memory and aging. The research shows that memory is not a single entity. Instead, it consists of many functions. Some change with age. Others remain stable throughout life. I describe how these changes can affect you in daily life and what you can do to minimize their impact and keep your memory functioning at its peak. The overall message of the book is positive. It indicates that adults of all ages can improve their memory ability.

A good memory is not something fixed that you have or don't have. Your memory for the past, as well as your memory for new information, depends on what you *do* to remember. Since most people don't know how they remember, I devote one chapter to helping you evaluate your memory. This process takes time, but I think you will find it interesting and revealing. It will also help you tailor your use of this book to your own needs, strengths, and weaknesses. In addition, I explain how to distinguish between occasional memory lapses and the more serious memory failures associated with specific diseases.

For lifelong memory maintenance, I describe techniques—called memory strategies—that can be applied to a variety of everyday memory tasks and offer practical suggestions for practicing them. As with any other skill, you will become proficient only if you practice the techniques. If you simply read the book without beginning to use the memory strategies every day, you can't expect your memory to improve.

If you envision yourself as someday becoming a memory expert who can learn 100 names in 20 minutes, this is not the book for you. Although many of the systems and techniques are the same, the focus here is on everyday situations. Reading this book will give you the tools for maximizing memory success. You will remember more and forget less.

1

What Is Memory?

Paul is a real estate broker. He keeps meticulous, organized records, but he rarely consults them. Off the top of his head, he can tell you the description, price range, size, layout, and location of hundreds of houses on the market, he knows the names of all the subdivisions in town, and he can direct you to any residential street in the area.

Martha wishes she had a good memory. If only she did, she believes, she could put off studying for her history test until a couple of nights before. Then she could sit down and memorize twenty-five important dates, six obscure treaties and their provisions, eight kings, and five reasons why the French Revolution took place.

Eric's family marvels at his memory. When he describes the battles he fought in during World War II, the family can hear the guns and see in vivid detail every hill, village, and soldier.

Joanne is convinced that her son has the worst memory in the world. She reminds him time and time again to make his bed in the morning, but when she confronts him with the tangles of covers on the floor, he shrugs apologetically and says, "Sorry, mom. I forgot."

George met Dave at a party for the first time in February. They chatted about their jobs and families. When they met again in April, Dave said, "Hi, George. How's the insurance business and how's your daughter Kathy doing." George was amazed. "Wow," he told Dave, "You have a fantastic memory."

Peter, who retired recently, is convinced that his memory is going bad. Several times lately, he's written an appointment on his calendar and then missed the appointment because he forgot to check the calendar.

We all know someone who we think has an excellent memory. Many of us wish, like Martha and Peter, that ours could be better. No matter who we are or what we do, life would be easier if only we had a good memory. We all fret at the people around us—our children, our colleagues, our parents, our spouse—whose "poor" memories make our life more difficult. And, if the forgetters around us—or we ourselves—happen to be middle-aged or older, we secretly worry that the memory lapses are an early sign of senility.

Memory in everyday life. It is not surprising that we are sensitive to changes in our memory ability and to memory lapses in those around us. After all, practically everything we do requires memory, whether we are trying to learn a new language, dance step, or job skill, studying for a test, or simply carrying out daily activities. Memory is involved whenever we recall an event or person we know, tell an amusing story to a friend, run errands, complete tasks, or make phone calls. Memory is involved whenever we drive, not only for finding our way around town but for performing the correct movements required to operate the car safely. Memory for language, vocabulary, and grammatical rules is required when we speak. In other words, memory is essential to every aspect of our work and social life, even to knowing who and where we are!

FACTORS THAT AFFECT MEMORY

Do some people just naturally have a good memory?

Why do we forget?

Can we improve our memory?

Why do we remember the name of our first grade teacher but forget our current neighbor's last name?

Do we remember only when we want to remember?

Does it really get harder to remember things as we get older or does it just seem that way?

The answer to these and many other questions people have about memory is the inevitable but unsatisfying, "It depends." Your memory power—the ability to memorize new material, to retain information for long time periods, and to recall things at will—depends on many factors. It depends on what you want to remember, on the circumstances in which you are asked to remember, and on your age, education, health, motivation, and other personal characteristics. Some of these are within your control and others are not. One fact that can be stated unequivocally is that people differ enormously in memory power.

Age

Age is related to memory performance throughout the lifespan. By the age of 7, children are equal to adults in their ability to remember five to ten pieces of information for a short time. But their long-term memory lags behind. It is not until they are 12 to 15 years old that children demonstrate memory capabilities similar to those of college students. Until then, children simply do not use the best methods for remembering. The same is true for many older people.

Just as with athletic ability, there are enormous individual variations in memory ability within each age level. Some 3-year-olds can memorize songs with ten verses while some 8-year-olds have trouble with three verses. At 80 years of age, the famous psychologist B. F. Skinner was still demonstrating intellectual acumen far above that of many younger people.

Fortunately, for most people, getting older does not lead to dramatic declines in memory power. The changes that do occur as you age can be minimized by strengthening the factors that *are* in your control. With training and practice, your memory ability can be substantially improved at any age. You can take greater advantage of your potential ability, which is probably much higher than your actual level of performance.

Education and Expertise

There is a relationship between educational level and memory skill. Higher education places large memory demands on students, and the memory skills required for studying last a long time because they are so well learned. Also, people with more education are likely to be engaged in occupations that require them to use their mental ability and are more likely, even in their leisure time, to pursue intellectually challenging activities. As a result, older people who are highly educated tend to show less memory decline than those with little education.

People who have mastered a subject or skill will learn new information in that area easily, because the new information fits into familiar patterns and relationships. When they need to recall those facts, many associations will bring them to mind.

Intelligence

Intelligent people usually have good memories. In fact, memory ability is regarded as one component of intelligence. If you have ever taken an I.Q. test, you know that having a good memory helps. Some parts of the test assess general information, and for those questions it is useful if you can remember how yeast works or the names of the last three presidents. Other parts measure memory directly. For example, the examiner might ask you to repeat a series of numbers backwards after you have heard them once.

High I.Q. is not enough, by itself, to guarantee a good memory for everything. Have you ever known an absent-minded professor who understands biophysics perfectly but always forgets his lunch? He is obviously brilliant, but he seems to have memory problems. The probable explanation for such behavior is that he remembers only what he wants to remember and what he pays attention to.

Self-Concept

If you don't think you'll be able to remember something, you are not likely to put forth the effort necessary to succeed. If you think you are going to be wrong, you won't make guesses about events you are trying to recall, even though your guesses could be correct. In addition, fear of failure can lead to excessive anxiety that gets in the way of clear thinking and further reduces performance. If you *think* that your memory is poor, it may eventually become that way because you won't bother to exercise your memory skills.

Health

Whether you are sick with something as minor as a cold or suffer from a chronic cardiovascular condition, your memory will be affected. Illness not only drains your mental energy, it isolates you from social contact that provides mental stimulation. Poor health and fatigue affect everyone's memory ability, but an older person is more likely than his younger counterpart to be ill or tired. Also, specific illnesses, such as Alzheimer's disease, can rob you of your memory.

Motivation and Effort

Day to day variations in memory, as well as differences in ability from one person to another, may be related to motivation and effort. Like self-concept and health, motivation and effort do not affect your basic competence but they do affect your performance. If you have to remember something that is not interesting to you, you may not try very hard. The typical teenager forgets to come home on time because he is not the least bit interested in remembering. But he can memorize a seemingly endless number of statistics about his favorite football team. Motivation is valuable because it drives you to make persistent efforts to remember. And whenever you put forth effort, you will usually achieve memory success.

Strategy Usage

Applying effective memory strategies will improve your memory. *Memory strategy* and *mnemonic* are terms used to describe any method or technique that enhances your ability to remember. They may be used when you are learning something new or when you are trying to recall something you already know.

Strategies can range from the simple, such as repeating a phone number five times, to the complex, such as creating a story that links several ideas you are trying to remember. Each individual has a set of strategies which he typically uses. Thus you might make a list of things to do (an external strategy) or you might mentally picture a courtroom to remind yourself to call your lawyer (an internal strategy). Those that have been practiced extensively will be chosen more often and will be vastly more effective than unfamiliar strategies.

Personal characteristics play a role in strategy selection. For example, some people are visualizers and some are verbalizers. If you are a *visualizer,* you use mental pictures to recall faces, information you've read, places you've been, or conversations. I am a *verbalizer,* so my natural tendency is to outline and organize information according to meaning or to use the first letters of words as cues for remembering long lists of information. I use mental pictures only to memorize something that is not easily described with words, such as an abstract fabric pattern or a face.

It takes effort for verbalizers to develop images. Some people tell me that they can never get pictures in their minds. They can't even picture their own faces without going to the mirror! This is the extreme, however; most verbalizers can improve their ability to visualize.

PREDICTING PERFORMANCE ON MEMORY TESTS

Even if factors such as self-concept and motivation could be assessed, it would still be difficult to predict your performance on a memory test. Many other variables, including the memory task itself and the testing situation, determine how much you will remember. Both of these variables also interact with personal characteristics.

If new information is presented rapidly, for example, an older person will not recall as much as a young person. If two people of the same age and intelligence are asked to recall the position of chess pieces on a board, a chess player will do better than his bridge-playing friend. If the test is to draw (from memory) the furniture in a room after it has been seen only once, a visualizer will have an advantage over a verbalizer.

The testing situation itself can affect performance. If you are not familiar with the setting or if you are ill-at-ease in the room, you may be tense and easily distracted by unfamiliar sights and sounds, so that you will not recall very much.

SPECIAL INDIVIDUALS

A *mnemonist* is someone who has a much greater range of memory skills and a much better memory than the average person. You may have seen mnemonists on television programs showing off their amazing skill, which, in many cases, depends on complex strategy systems they have practiced and perfected.

It is apparent that the mnemonist's systematic and efficient application of strategies greatly increases the amount of information he can remember. But no single system can encompass all kinds of memory tasks, and remembering will occur only when it is applied. Mnemonists certainly cannot remember everything they do, hear, or read. In some cases, a mnemonist may have one particular method so perfected that he cannot memorize anything that does not fit it. For instance, in *The Mind of a Mnemonist*, A. R. Luria, a famous scholar of memory, described the ability of "S" to use mental images to recall hundreds of words, numbers, letters, or simple pictures. He had tremendous memory power. But "S" relied so exclusively on a particular type of imagery that problems occurred. He could not recall faces because he was too sensitive to minute changes in expression. He was very poor at logical organization of words and could not integrate paragraphs to remember their overall meaning.

A person with a *photographic memory* can hold an exact image of an entire page in his mind. But this extreme visualizing skill is very rare. It is more common in children than in adults because as we grow up we tend to think more in terms of words rather than pictures.

The term *idiot savant* is used to refer to people who are mentally retarded but who have mastered some single, particular kind of intellectual or artistic skill. You may have read about a retarded man who could tell what the weather had been on any day for the last thirty years, or the retarded twins who did complex mathematical calculations to answer calendar questions. In both cases, only that one skill was performed well. There are no cogent explanations for the idiot savant phenomenon. Some people believe that one area of the brain may have been overdeveloped to the detriment of others.

When a person suffers from *amnesia,* usually the result of a head injury or trauma, he may forget specific events from the past and/or be unable to learn new information, but he will do as well as a normal person on those parts of an I.Q. test that require no memory skill.

MEMORY RESEARCH

Memory has interested philosophers, scientists, and scholars for centuries, but it is only in the last 100 years, since the field of psychology emerged, that memory has been investigated systematically in the laboratory. A basic goal of the research is to try to isolate and describe the factors that affect memory. By testing a person's ability to perform specific memory tasks, scientists hope to learn how a certain factor, such as age, influences his mental activity when he remembers.

A second goal is to describe the relationship between a person's mental memory activity and his actual memory performance, such as how much he remembers, how much time it takes him to remember, and how durable the memories are.

Since science has not yet advanced to the point of knowing the actual physical or chemical changes that occur in the brain when information is stored, mental activity cannot be studied directly. Instead it must be inferred from the way people perform on memory tests. If, for example, a person is asked to remember a list of words and he recalls the words in related pairs (STEREO and PIANO, ELEPHANT and GIRAFFE), the experimenter can infer that association was part of the individual's memory activity.

Episodic and Semantic Memory

Psychologists categorize memory tasks into two types: episodic and semantic. *Episodic memory* is memory for specific events or for information learned at a specific time and place. *Semantic memory* refers to your memory for words, concepts, and categories.

Episodic memory is involved when you remember to attend a business luncheon or when you recall the time you fell from a tree at age 7 and broke your arm. It is tested in the typical memory experiment, in which participants are required to look at a list of words for a specific time and then try to recall those words.

Although most laboratory studies of memory involve episodic memory, much of your everyday usage of mental skills requires semantic memory. You speak and write sentences without realizing that you are relying on memory for the meanings of the words and concepts that the sentences convey. The semantic memory system is organized so that words or concepts that have similar meanings (river and stream) are called into mind at the same time. World knowledge, such as the name of the president of the United States, or the answer to the problem *2+2,* is also part of semantic memory.

The distinction between episodic and semantic memory is useful, but the two do not operate independently; both types are involved whenever you need to remember something. If you were asked to memorize thirty words in the laboratory, a task that is based on episodic memory, you would probably use your semantic memory knowledge to group those with similar meanings so that you could recall more of them. Similarly, although semantic memory for language is acquired gradually, you may recall the specific place and time that you first understood a concept.

THREE STAGES OF MEMORY

Memory is typically characterized by psychologists as a three-stage process: learning, retention, and recall. Most people use the word "remembering" to refer to all three.

Learning

Learning is the first stage in the memory process—trying to get information into your mind for the first time. It is also called *encoding* or *acquisition*. There are two kinds of learning: intentional and incidental.

INTENTIONAL LEARNING

Learning is intentional when you make a deliberate effort to learn something new. When you meet someone and remember his name, when you read a company's annual report and remember relevant figures, when your boss asks you to do certain tasks and you keep them in mind until you complete them—these are examples of intentional learning. Because of your conscious effort to learn something, you will probably use memory strategies, though you may not be aware of doing so.

Researchers study the use of strategies to develop a greater understanding of how memory works. Can you improve your memory? Yes, though your degree of success will be related to your use of memory strategies. Why can't older people remember as well as younger people? Again, part of the answer seems to be that older people do not use strategies as effectively as younger people do.

For any individual, the best strategies are those that lead to the greatest recall. Some strategies work well for everyone. In a typical laboratory investigation of memory, the experimenter presents a series of words, one by one on slides and afterwards asks the participant to write down the ones he remembers. The words are names of animals, furniture, vehicles, and foods. Researchers have learned that the person who systematically organizes the information in his head will write the animal names he can remember, the furniture, the vehicles, and the foods. People who organize information in this way will almost always recall more words than those who do not.

Research evidence shows that, in general, older people learn at a slower rate than younger people. But at any age, those who use good strategies need fewer study periods to master new material.

INCIDENTAL LEARNING

Incidental memory comes into play when you recall information you did not try to remember in the first place. Suppose, for example, that you and your colleagues are discussing last night's basketball game. When you were watching the game, you didn't make any conscious effort to remember it. But now you would like to remember what happened.

The crucial factors for successful incidental recall are attention and mental activity. Let us assume that none of you used any memory strategies during the game. If you sat there thinking about a report you had to write, you probably won't be able to remember much of the game. But if your colleagues paid attention to team members setting up plays, admired the ball handling, and applauded the high scorer, their later recall of the game is likely to be excellent. They will remember details because they were attentive and, more important, because they noted the meaning of what was happening. Even though none of you intended to learn, those who paid attention encoded a great deal.

In a typical investigation of incidental learning, the experimenter asks participants to perform a task involving a set of information, but they are not told that they will have to recall the information. For example, Group A is asked to sort pictures of common objects (desk supplies, kitchen utensils, furniture) according to the rooms in which the items would normally be found. Group B is asked to sort the same pictures according to the first letter in the name of the object. After sorting, both groups write down the names of the objects they remember. Members of Group A have better recall in this kind of test because their sorting task requires them to pay attention to the meaning, or purpose, of the objects.

When people cannot recall something learned incidentally, they commonly call it "forgetting." If your colleagues spend time talking about an especially good play in the basketball game, and you don't remember it, you may feel frustrated and say to yourself, "Darn! Why did I forget that play?" Technically, though, you didn't forget because you never noticed it in the first place. Nevertheless, throughout this book I use the term "forgetting" as most people do, to refer to all mistakes in remembering information to which you have been exposed.

Retention

Retention is the storage of what has been learned. Important issues in the study of memory storage are time (how long can you retain information?), capacity (how much information can you retain?), and forgetting (how does forgetting occur after storage?).

The two main types of storage evaluated by psychologists are called immediate memory and long-term memory. Each differs in terms of retention time, capacity, and forgetting.

IMMEDIATE MEMORY

You retain information in immediate, or short-term memory, for as long as you pay attention to it and for up to one minute after you shift attention. You use immediate memory when you look up a phone number and then dial it or when you meet a new employee and remember the name just long enough to make a personnel file. Immediate memory ability does not seem to decline with age.

This storage system has a limited capacity—about seven items. It's handy, then, that phone numbers contain seven digits. One reason that many people don't like nine-digit zip codes is that they exceed short-term capacity.

The critical limit on immediate memory is the number of items—the size of each item is not an issue. If all of the phone numbers in your office begin with 258, the number 258-6731 involves only five items of information, because the three-digit exchange is so familiar that your mind treats it as one item of information.

Forgetting occurs in short-term storage primarily through a process of displacement. If a string of digits or words exceeds short-term memory limits, the last few items in the series can displace the earlier ones. Whenever you focus your attention on additional information, the old information is pushed out to make way for the new. You may have just looked up an address to write it on an envelope, but when someone walks in and asks you to lunch, you forget the address. There isn't enough room for both sets of information, so your immediate memory focuses on the one that entered your mind most recently. Interruptions play havoc with immediate memory.

LONG-TERM MEMORY

Anything that you remember for more than one minute is committed to long-term memory. Information becomes stored in long-term memory if it is learned very well in the first place. Here is where effective memory strategies make a difference. Taking notes during an interesting lecture may be the key to retaining the information in your long-term memory. Making presentations about your trip to India will help you recall the details of the trip for many years to come.

Whereas immediate memory has a limited capacity, long-term memory has no known limits. Throughout your life, you will continue to learn new things and retain them for long periods of time. Presumably, then, older people should have a large knowledge base of information acquired over a lifetime, much larger than that of younger people. We have no way of knowing whether this is the case.

If there are no limits, why does forgetting occur? One theory is that your memories gradually decay until they are no longer clear. They fade, like a photograph exposed to the sun, until the details are lost. To confirm that decay takes place, scientists would have to understand what actually happens within or among the cells of a person's brain when a memory is stored. So far, this has not been accomplished.

Many scholars take a different approach and claim that forgetting never occurs in long-term memory. Instead, they say, the information is retained forever; it just may not be accessible because you don't know how to search and find everything that has been stored. According to this point of view, forgetting occurs only because you haven't been given useful cues or questions to assist the search process. Psychoanalysis is based on the belief that the right kinds of questions can bring back to mind formative childhood events that are retained in memory but are not immediately accessible.

HOW RETENTION IS STUDIED

Retention—memory storage—is studied by looking at three factors: forgetting rates, savings, and interference.

In a typical retention experiment the participant studies approximately thirty words until he can recall all of them. To examine his rate of forgetting, he is asked to remember the words at intervals from one to forty-eight hours later, without seeing them again. Generally speaking, the rate of forgetting is fairly rapid over the first twelve hours and slows down thereafter. Forgetting rates are usually similar for older and younger people, and there is typically less forgetting if the words are *overlearned,* that is, if they are studied repeatedly even after they have been committed to memory.

In experiments on savings, the participant studies the words once. After he has forgotten many of them, he studies the same words to see how quickly he can learn them the second time. The information retained from initial learning is his savings. If anything is saved—stored in long-term memory—the rate of learning is faster the second time. If you learned French in high school and take a refresher course years later, you should learn it faster the second time because of savings.

Interference may also affect retention. Interference is difficulty in recalling particular information because it is similar, but not the same as, something stored earlier. Your familiarity with French grammar, for example, may interfere with learning the grammar of another Romance language.

Recall

Recall, or retrieval, is the stage in which you try to bring back to mind information that has been learned and retained. Memory awareness is high at this stage; you notice your memory failures most often during recall. The most important factors affecting recall are the strategies you have used during learning, the number of cues available, and the recall context.

Research on the value of cues as memory aids shows that older adults need more cues or memory supports for recall than younger people do. Psychologists test the effect of memory cues on the ability to recall by constructing tests that vary only in the number of cues provided. As you would expect, with less memory support, recall is more difficult. To improve your recall, the best strategy is to provide yourself with cues.

FREE RECALL

If someone asked you the details of a board meeting you attended a few days ago, and you had not taken notes at the meeting, you would depend on free recall, which requires an open-ended search through memory. In a free recall test, there are no cues. The experimenter simply shows you a list of words and asks you to remember them.

CUED RECALL

If you had an agenda for the board meeting, you would have some cues to help you remember. Reading the agenda might help you remember the discussion and vote for each agenda item. On a cued recall test, the cues set some limits and guide the search process.

RECOGNITION

When you enter a room full of people, it is relatively easy to recognize the faces of those you have met previously. Recognition, then, provides total recall support because the item you have to remember is in front of you. Recognition is usually the easiest type of recall test. The information that you have learned is presented to you along with new information, and you simply have to recognize the old, previously learned items.

RECALL CONTEXT

The closer that you can approximate the context in which something was learned, the more likely you will be able to recall it. If you return to the same room where you heard a speech, you will probably remember it better than you would in your office. On the other hand, even if you see and recognize the same bank teller every time you make a deposit, you may not recognize her at the post office because she would be out of context.

Memories also have emotional contexts. You have a better chance of recalling a song if you can reinstate the mood you were in when you first heard it. When you are depressed, memories from previous bouts of depression are likely to come back because those old feelings are associated with your present mood.

Your physical state also has an effect. If you learn something under the influence of drugs, you will recall it better when you are in the same condition. There is a classic story that illustrates this. An alcoholic worked as a forklift operator for twenty-five years. He had gained experience on the job and was very efficient with his machine. His alcoholism finally got so bad that his family insisted that he "dry out." After his rehabilitation, he returned to work only to find that he was fumbling around. He had learned to operate the machine "under the influence" and now that he was sober, he couldn't remember how!

It will be easier to reinstate the learning context in the presence of recall cues that remind you of that context. In other words, the associations you make when you learn something are the best associations to think about again when you recall it. In a typical study of this phenomenon, a person is asked to remember the underlined words in a sentence, such as "The child carried a teddy bear along the river bank." Later, when tested for recall of the underlined words BEAR and BANK, he will remember them more readily if he is aided by the cues "child" and "river." If the cues are "grizzly" and "money" (normally good associations for "bear" and "bank"), he will not do as well.

RECONSTRUCTION

Every time you recall something, your memory for that information changes through a process called reconstruction. New associations and cues are added and become part of the context in which recall occurred. For example, each time you tell someone the story about your Grand Canyon vacation, you add a little twist to it to make the story more interesting. This is perfectly legitimate among friends. Over time, however, the story changes. The new information becomes integrated with your initial memories. By the time you have told it fifteen times, the story may be very different from what actually occurred!

The process of reconstruction is demonstrated most dramatically in investigations of eyewitness testimony. An investigator showed three groups of people the *same pictures* of a car accident and asked them various questions about the accident. Group A and Group B were asked, respectively, "About how fast were the cars going when they bumped?" and "About how fast were the cars going when they collided?" Group C was asked, "About how fast were the cars going when they smashed?" One week later all the participants were asked, "How fast were the cars going?" Those in Group C consistently reported greater speeds. They apparently inferred from the word "smashed" that the cars were going very fast, and this inference became part of their memory of the accident. It is astonishing that such a small thing as the rephrasing of a question could have such an impact on recall.

INDIVIDUAL DIFFERENCES IN MEMORY

An individual's memory success may vary from one stage of memory to another. For instance, Eric's recall of war events is remarkable, but he may find that learning new information is difficult and painstaking because his learning strategies are poor. Once Martha applies herself, she may be able to memorize many historical facts for her test. But after the test when her motivation is gone, she may no longer retain them.

Such variations in memory skill are present throughout the life span, so you should not expect that aging will have the same impact on everyone. Although research evidence shows age-related changes in some aspects of memory, variability among individuals actually increases with age, so that the difference between the best and worst memorizers in their seventies is larger than the difference between the best and worst memorizers in their twenties.

2

What Happens to Memory as You Grow Older

There is a classic joke about aging . . . you've probably heard it before: "There are three things that happen when you get older. One, you lose your memory, and . . . uh . . . I forgot the other two!"

I hear remarks like that all the time from middle-aged and older adults. The truth is that memory mistakes are common at all ages although the number and kind of memory errors you make may change as you get older.

ABILITIES THAT CHANGE

Researchers investigating this problem have found the following changes to be part of the normal aging process:

Thinking is slower.

The best memory strategies are used less.

Paying attention and ignoring distractions become more difficult.
Learning something new takes more time.
More cues are needed to recall something previously learned.

Thinking is Slower

The speed with which you perform nearly every thinking, memory, and problem-solving task decreases as you get older. This slowing appears to affect everyone and is related to a general age-associated decline in reaction time. I'm sure you have heard about athletes who are "over the hill" at 35. They don't react as quickly—they don't jump, begin to run, raise their gloves, or kick as quickly as they did in their youth. Although your memory is definitely not over the hill at age 35, learning, strategy application, rehearsal, search, and recall all take longer as you get older.

SLOWING IN DAILY LIFE

Although the impact of slowing on everyday memory has not been examined systematically, anecdotal evidence from middle-aged and older persons confirms that slowing occurs, and the memory lapses that annoy or alarm many people are often related to it. Slower thinking shows up when you have to give an immediate reaction to a problem, and it has the greatest impact when the situation or problem is new and complex.

Suppose, for example, that you get a call at home Friday evening from a colleague in another city, who asks you to speak at a conference on Monday because the scheduled speaker has been taken ill. Before you give him your decision, which he needs immediately, you have to remember and evaluate a number of details quickly. What do you have on your calendar for Monday? Do you have any files on the topic? Is there a convenient flight so that you don't have to miss Sunday's golf tournament? Is there other business you can conduct in that city to make the trip worthwhile? This type of memory task becomes harder as you get older.

Slower thinking also means that a word or name doesn't come to mind as quickly as before. You meet a friend at a concert whom you haven't seen for a long time and have trouble remembering his name. A TV announcer gives an address rapidly and the message is over before you have had a chance to memorize it. When you don't have your appointment book with you, it takes you some time to reconstruct your week. Younger people, too, may take a few minutes to recall such information, but, on the average, you will find that recall takes longer as you get older.

RESEARCH EVIDENCE

A typical experiment related to the impact of slowing on memory involves asking two groups of subjects (one of college students and one of people over 60) to remember words presented on slides at a controlled rate. The experimenter can pace the slides either very rapidly (one slide every two seconds), slowly (one slide every eight seconds), or he can present each slide when the participant says he is ready (self-paced). Age-related differences in scores are generally smaller when learning is self-paced, indicating that the presentation rate affects older adults more than younger ones.

Other evidence for the effects of slowing comes from an experiment in which subjects were asked to study paired words, such as APPLE-TABLE, CHAIR-CAR, BOOK-GLOVE. Then they were shown one word from each pair and asked to recall the other word as a response. The goal was 10 correct responses. When the time allowed for each response was short (2.2 seconds), the younger group required about eight practice periods and the older group needed twenty-three practice periods. With 6.6 seconds to respond, the "young" reached the goal after seven practice periods and the "old" after nine practice periods. The older people eventually learned the words as well as the students; they just needed more time to recall what they had learned.

EXPLANATION

Why does slowing occur? Some psychologists think that older people are slower because they are more cautious. They take longer to make decisions and to reach conclusions because they do not want to make errors. Others believe that physiological changes result in slower transmission of information in the brain. These changes include loss of nerve cells, reduced flow of blood and oxygen to the brain, reduced electrical activity (indicated by slower EEG patterns), and changes in the properties of nerve cells. There is no doubt these changes occur, but scientists have not determined their impact on memory.

HOW TO MAINTAIN ABILITIES

Although there may be no direct way to speed up the functioning of your brain, the impact of slowing will be minimized with practice, familiarity, and high motivation.

Card sorting studies illustrate the benefits of familiarity. The cards used in these experiments are of varying colors and have different shapes drawn on them. Subjects are asked to sort the cards five times according to instructions given. The experimenter shuffles the cards between sortings. Subjects in Group A are told each time to put all green cards into one pile and all others into another pile. Subjects in Group B are also asked, on the first sorting, to divide the cards into a green and a non-green pile. The second time, however, members of Group B have to sort into six piles according to six shapes drawn on the cards. The rules change for each subsequent sorting. Age differences in sorting speed are smaller when the rule remains the same each time the cards are sorted. In other words, familiarity with the rule reduces the impact of slowing.

Years of practice can also compensate for memory slowdown. In an investigation of memory functions required for playing chess, skilled older players were just as likely to select correct moves as skilled younger players, but the older players' recall of the location of specific chess pieces on the board was poorer than that of their young competitors. Because they were more experienced, the older players were able to use more efficient methods for scanning and noting patterns of pieces on the board before each play. Evidently, their years of practice helped them locate pieces quickly and select the correct moves.

The importance of familiarity and practice has been demonstrated in the workplace as well. The experienced older worker can finish a task as rapidly as a younger colleague because he has learned how to combine or simplify steps. In addition, if an activity is so highly practiced that it can be performed without a great deal of mental effort, slowing should not have much impact on the ability to do that task. An older, experienced bank teller, for instance, can count money rapidly and can quickly process forms for a bank transaction. An inexperienced teller of the same age will work more slowly.

If motivation is high, slowing has less impact. People who choose the words they need to learn in a memory experiment often learn faster than people who are given no choice. High motivation may provide the extra push to perform quickly regardless of age.

Effective Strategies Are Used Less Often

Older people are less likely than younger to use strategies such as organization, association, or imagery, and, as a result, they tend to have lower scores on memory tests. It is not clear whether older people do not use these strategies at all or whether they simply do not apply them systematically and efficiently.

STRATEGY USE IN DAILY LIFE

Memory strategies can be used to remember names, the highlights of a newspaper article, your medication schedule, the points you want to make in a speech, or the instructions for your new camera. You can remember anything better when you use effective strategies. Without them, you will find yourself forgetting details you thought you knew, and you will need a great deal longer to learn new information.

RESEARCH EVIDENCE

After participating in studies that require them to memorize a list of words, younger adults are more likely to report that they envisioned a picture to go with each word. If the list contains related words (CHAIR, DOG, ORANGE, TABLE, CAT, APPLE), younger adults are more likely to rehearse and recall the related words together. As a result, the younger group has higher scores.

On some memory tests, a word to be memorized is presented along with questions that may be related to the meaning of the word or to its sound. For example, a question for PURSE might be, "Is this something a girl would carry to school or something used in the kitchen?" Or, "Does this word rhyme with nurse or cart?" When the questions are related to the meaning of the word, the young remember more of the words, making it appear that they are better at developing meaningful word associations, at least on memory tests.

EXPLANATION

One reason older people may not use memory strategies effectively is that the slowing process, described earlier, makes using them more difficult. When information is presented rapidly, older people may not have enough time to organize it.

In a study demonstrating the impact of slowing, people were asked to read sentences and remember a single underlined word in each sentence. In the recall test, the sentences were presented with the underlined words missing. The younger subjects remembered more words than the older ones because they associated the words with other information in the sentences. In a follow-up study that tested only the younger group, the intervals between sentence presentations were cut in half, from eight seconds to four seconds. In this test the younger people performed at the same level as the older people had done in the first study; apparently, the shorter interval was not long enough for effective strategy usage.

Some psychologists feel that changes in educational methods may be responsible, in part, for older people's application of fewer memory techniques. The older generation learned primarily by rote, whereas later on, students were taught to note meaning and association, techniques that can be applied to memory tests.

College students, who constitute the pool of young volunteers for memory research, have an "occupation" requiring considerable memorization. Older people may not use the best methods for remembering simply because they don't have to and, as a result, get out of practice. This disuse hypothesis is supported by evidence that mentally alert adults placed in nursing homes because of physical disabilities sometimes start losing their mental ability because they lack intellectual stimulation.

HOW TO MAINTAIN ABILITIES

The best way to keep your memory in shape is to continually challenge it. Older adults who use appropriate memorizing methods are usually those who have remained intellectually active. Their memory demands and their need for strategies have not decreased with age.

If you are out of the habit of using memory strategies, or never used them in the first place, you will find it reassuring to know that age will not stand in your way. You may not regain memory performance equal to that of your younger years, but you can expect training and practice to improve your memory abilities by as much as 50 percent.

Maintaining Attention Becomes Difficult

You will find it more difficult to pay attention and ignore distractions as you get older. You will also have trouble shifting your attention back and forth rapidly between two tasks or following two conversations at the same time. Reductions in concentration make it harder to remember. As with other factors that affect memory, the ability to pay attention varies from person to person. Even though my friend Catherine is only 36, she finds it almost impossible to read the newspaper while she's listening to the news. I can easily concentrate on two or three tasks, such as writing a computer program and helping my 6-year-old daughter read a book, at the same time.

PAYING ATTENTION IN DAILY LIFE

If you have ever been talking with friends at a party and then become aware of an interesting conversation nearby, you will understand the problem of trying to pay attention to two things at once. When you are older, you may have to limit yourself to following only one conversation or else you will have trouble remembering either of them. In addition, you may find yourself easily distracted by events or people around you. It will be difficult, for example, to concentrate on a movie while people around you are talking.

It's not only external distractions that cause memory problems. You have an attention problem when you can't remember where you put your glasses—you were probably thinking about something else. Or when you set off down the hall to do something and don't remember what you started to do—you probably let your mind wander. Everyone experiences such lapses in attention, but they become more common as people get older. You are less likely to pay attention to the routine aspects of your daily life, and that's why it is so easy to misplace your keys.

RESEARCH EVIDENCE

The ability to pay attention is sometimes tested with listening tasks. The subject wears earphones so that different words can be recited into each ear. In one ear he hears JOB . . . CART . . . HORSE . . . RECORD, and in the other ear he hears FLOOR . . . GLASS . . . SHIP . . . GOAT. Older people tend to focus on one ear and forget the words the other ear hears. Young people find it easier to keep track of and remember both sets of words.

Divided attention tests demonstrate that it is relatively hard for older people to concentrate on one task when they are distracted. In one version of this type of test, the participant studies a group of pictures for five minutes. His goal is to recall the pictures three minutes later, but during the three minute interval, he has to count backwards. The new task requires him to divide his attention between reviewing the pictures mentally and counting. Older people are bothered more by the distraction of counting and perform considerably worse than younger people.

The ability to focus on important information also diminishes with age. In a typical experiment, subjects are asked to remember only the central object in each of a series of pictures. One picture, for example, might show a chair in the center of a room full of furniture, people, and knick knacks. Older people find it more difficult to focus attention on the central object and ignore or filter out irrelevant details in the picture. They remember the people or the knick knacks and forget the chair.

EXPLANATION

Some researchers believe that older people are simply less interested in performing well on these kinds of tests and therefore do not concentrate. The research evidence available so far does not indicate whether or not motivation is a critical factor.

An alternate explanation focuses on attentional capacity itself. Attention has limits; you cannot attend simultaneously to everything around you. To remember, you must attend selectively to whatever it is that you want to learn. Some scholars believe that older people cannot focus attention on as much information as young people. It is also possible that aging affects the ability to identify and attend to exactly what needs to be remembered and to ignore all extraneous details.

HOW TO MAINTAIN ABILITIES

In Chapter 8, I will describe ways to improve your attention and concentration skills. For now, I will say only that you need to be very aware of whether or not you are focusing on your present activity. Make an effort to center your mind on the task at hand. Call yourself back to attention whenever you notice that your mind is wandering.

Learning Takes Longer

It will probably take longer to learn something new when you are older. If you are unwilling to devote this extra time or if you become overly anxious because you aren't learning as quickly as you think you should, you may have difficulty learning.

TAKING LONGER TO LEARN IN DAILY LIFE

As you get older, you will need more practice and review to acquire job skills. It will take you longer to learn where items are located in a new house after you move. If you decide to learn a new language, you will have to allow more time to review and think about the grammar, vocabulary, and idioms. You will have to study longer and harder if you return to school as an older student.

RESEARCH EVIDENCE

In a typical experiment, the subject is shown line drawings of 40 common objects and is told that he will have to recall 32 of them. The experimenter gives him several study periods, each followed by a recall test, until he achieves a score of 32 correct on one test. Older people need from two to ten more study periods than younger people.

More time is needed for complex learning also, as the following study demonstrates. Subjects are shown cut out letters varying in size, texture, color, and shape. Their goal is to identify the object characteristic—such as blue—that has been arbitrarily selected as "correct" by the experimenter. On the first trial the participant sees, for example, a large, soft, blue **O** and a small, hard, green **X**, and he is asked to choose one of the two letters. The next pair might be a small, hard, blue **O** and a large, soft, green **X**. The correct answer is always the blue letter. Older people require considerably more trials than younger people to consistently select the correct answer.

EXPLANATION

Slower learning is a natural consequence of the many age-related changes in intellectual ability. As you grow older, it starts taking longer to learn new information because you may not be paying attention, because your mind works a little more slowly, and because you don't use effective memory strategies as often.

HOW TO MAINTAIN ABILITIES

Take your time. Practice and use good memory techniques, which will help you learn faster. Don't get overly anxious if learning is slower or more difficult than it used to be.

More Memory Cues Are Needed

A cue can be a word, picture, smell, song, or anything related to or associated with information or events to be remembered. When a cue is available, it aids recall. With more cues, more support, and more information available, age differences in memory performance are smaller.

Suppose that you are attending a convention and see Jerry Green's name on the program. You've met Mr. Green before, but cannot envision his face. If you sit quietly and search through your mind, you may be able to remember what he looks like. This approach uses no cues. Instead, you could try to imagine him standing by the registration desk at the hotel where you last saw him. This uses the setting of your last meeting as a cue. Or you could do nothing now and hope that you recognize him when you see him. The third approach provides complete information, the actual face, to support your memory.

MEMORY CUES IN DAILY LIFE

Even though everyone relies on cues to jog their memory, you'll probably need them more as you get older. To remember someone's name, you may have to think about where you last saw him and about your conversation. The situation and the conversation will serve as cues to help you to remember the name.

Sandy and her mother came across an old photograph of the two of them in formal dress. The clothes and the decorations in the background immediately reminded Sandy of the occasion. "That was taken at Aunt Ellen and Uncle Gary's party," she said to her mother. "Remember?" But her mother, who had been to many of their parties over the years, needed more cues. "Which party?" she asked. "Oh, you know," Sandy responded. "The one at the Hilton when Randy graduated from law school and Dad couldn't dance because he had a broken ankle, and the Myers surprised everyone by driving up from Florida." "Oh," said her mother, "*that* party. Now I remember!"

You may need more cues to learn something new.

Dan and his grandson were tourists in a city neither of them had been to before. The youngster learned his way around the neighborhood of their hotel very quickly with the help of a few cues—a bakery around the corner, a taxi stand in the middle of the block, a building with a distinctive facade on the next street. Dan eventually got oriented, but he needed to recognize many of the buildings on nearby streets before he knew where he was.

Luckily, cues are often available in everyday circumstances. You can easily identify a person you always see in the same context—the office, library, or neighborhood; the context is your cue. As you drive around a city, there are street signs to cue your spatial memory. When your boss asks you to show him a report, he cues you with the date, the topic, or the name of the person to whom it was addressed.

RESEARCH EVIDENCE

Two groups of subjects were asked to memorize 40 words, called "target words." One group was then given a recognition test, in which each of the target words was presented along with new words, called "distractors." Subjects were asked to circle the words they remembered from the original list. The second group was given a cued recall test, in which a related cue was provided for each of the target words, though the original word itself was not present. For example, when the target word was MOON, the cue was "sky." On the recognition test, older people remembered as many words as the younger people (about 37). On the cued recall test, however, with less support, the older participants recalled substantially fewer items (about 15 compared to 23).

Another study demonstrated that for older adults, new cues are not as much help as those available when the target words are learned initially. For this test, the experimenter presented a target word, for example SUN, accompanied by a cue: the sun is "something in the sky" or "a word that rhymes with run." When the same cues (sky or run) were provided again during recall, the older participants remembered many more words than when new cues were given. The young people scored almost as well with new cues as with familiar ones.

EXPLANATION

Older people may sometimes depend more on cues because they simply haven't learned the information very well. When you learn something thoroughly, you can recall it without retrieval support, but if you don't know it well, you need cues to bring it back to mind.

Strangely enough, older people perform better on recognition tests than on recall tests, even when recognition is difficult (with many distractor words) and recall is easy (with relatively few words to remember). The young do better on easy recall and easy recognition tests than on hard versions of either. Psychologists think this occurs because recall tests are more difficult; you have to search for a word *and* recognize it when it comes to mind.

HOW TO MAINTAIN ABILITIES

Be aware of your need for cues as you get older and learn how to use them. Even if you are relatively young, make it a habit to use cues frequently so that you don't have to overload your memory. Use single words, or pictures cut from a magazine (taped to your mirror or refrigerator, if necessary) that cue you to do errands or take your medicines. If you want to tell a friend about a program you saw on television, jot down a few notes about the main points to remind yourself of the entire program.

When you are trying to learn new information, whether it is a poem or the procedure for operating a film projector, look for something that can be used as a cue. For the poem, you could write rhyming or key words on notecards. With the projector, use the diagram on the side of the machine to help you remember the order of operation. If there is no diagram, you could memorize the number of steps in the directions as a cue, so that you won't omit any. Or you could visualize the whole process in your mind, one step after another, and use this visualization as your cue.

The best cues are those that were in the environment when you learned that information. Any cue that helps you reinstate the learning conditions in your mind will facilitate recall.

ABILITIES THAT DO NOT CHANGE

Memory remains relatively stable throughout life in the following areas:

> Immediate memory
> Recall of world knowledge
> Susceptibility to interference
> Forgetting rates
> Search processes

Immediate Memory

Immediate, or short-term memory, in which you can retain about seven items of information for a minute or so, does not decline with age. As long as you are not interrupted, you should be able to recall five to nine words or numbers immediately after you hear them.

IMMEDIATE MEMORY IN DAILY LIFE

You should be able to look up a telephone number, walk into the next room, and dial it just as easily at age 65 as you did at age 30. When you are introduced to someone, it should be as easy as ever to remember the name shortly thereafter (as long as you bothered to listen). When you pause in a conversation to eat a bite of food or take a drink, you should be able to continue the conversation without forgetting what you were talking about. When your secretary comes into your office to tell you about two or three appointments, you should be able to write the schedule down immediately after hearing it, no matter how old you are.

RESEARCH EVIDENCE

To investigate immediate memory, psychologists ask people to memorize items in order. When the goal is to remember five digits or seven words in a row, people in their sixties perform as well as people in their twenties.

Immediate memory is also examined by giving participants fifteen or twenty words to recall. If the memory test is given right away, the last few words should be in immediate memory. Many investigations have shown that age does not affect memory for those last few items.

World Knowledge

World knowledge is information that is extremely familiar because you read, hear, see, or think about it frequently. You are exposed to world knowledge so many times and in so many ways that you cannot say exactly when or where you learned it. You probably cannot remember, for example, when you first heard of the Olympics. Memory for world knowledge is called, technically, semantic memory. It is the ability to remember information that is not tied to a specific time or event.

You use semantic memory to remember the answers for simple arithmetic problems, the names of recent presidents or professional athletes, the titles of popular TV programs, the birthdates of family members, and the route to work in the morning. Semantic memory is also used to retain language itself. You may not think that you use memory to speak or to get to your office. But in a broad sense, you do.

Your ability to retain well-learned and familiar world knowledge does not change with age. In fact, you may score higher on tests of world knowledge as you get older.

WORLD KNOWLEDGE IN DAILY LIFE

When an older person describes the details of his younger years, he is recounting well-learned information. He might talk about what his first wife looked like, how she dressed, what she liked to do, and what they argued about. This information, associated with many friends, places, and situations, is part of semantic memory and accurately reflects the flavor and character of their lives together. His descriptions of specific events may or may not be precise; there is no way of knowing. I've certainly heard my relatives embellish stories from our past!

Semantic memory is also involved for work-related skills, which are usually not learned at a specific time and place, but are acquired through experience, review, and adaptation. The same is true for learning your way around office buildings, cities, supermarkets, and parks, which you do gradually and at your own pace. Eventually you can drive around town or do a job without even thinking about it.

Similarly, you retain well-learned and oft-repeated motor activities, such as riding a bicycle, ice skating, or typing, in semantic memory. When the typewriter comes out of the closet after years of disuse, you find that although you cannot type as rapidly as you did five years before, you know where the keys are and what basic movements are needed. Such skills are highly overlearned because you review and practice them regularly even after you are proficient. Overlearning makes any kind of information resistant to forgetting.

RESEARCH EVIDENCE

In studies of world knowledge, people are asked to recall names, faces, or facts from the past—information that is generally known to the public. Typical questions might be "Who played the male lead in 'On Golden Pond'?" and "Who was shot by Lee Harvey Oswald in Dallas?" Although the results of this research have been mixed, most of the studies show no age decline. There is some controversy over the research findings because it is difficult to ensure that the names, faces, or facts were *ever* learned by a particular individual.

Studies of intelligence provide stronger evidence for a lack of age difference in world knowledge. Older people score as well as younger on intelligence tests measuring vocabulary, reading comprehension, simple mathematical skills, and general information (where does paper come from? what are the colors in the American flag?). These tests measure skills and knowledge that have been acquired through repeated experience in the world and thus involve semantic memory. Because knowledge accumulates over a lifetime, performance on intelligence tests of this type sometimes increases with age.

Susceptibility to Interference

Do you find it difficult to learn a new way to do a well-practiced task? If so, your original learning is interfering with new learning. Do you find it difficult to remember what you said to a friend on the phone in the morning if you talked to him again in the afternoon? If so, your second conversation is interfering with your memory for the first. Interference in older people has been examined in both of these kinds of situations, and the data indicate that the young and old are equally susceptible to interference.

INTERFERENCE IN DAILY LIFE

Imagine yourself at the office Christmas party. You have just joined the firm in the last month and you do not know many people, but a colleague is introducing you to everyone who comes over to talk. The names you commit to memory early in the evening will interfere with your attempts to learn those you hear later. Similarly, as you meet more and more people, you will forget the names you heard previously if you made no special effort to memorize them. Even though you are clearly forgetting because of interference, it is reassuring to know that the degree of forgetting will not increase with age.

Motor skills are especially susceptible to interference. If you have ever tried to change a stroke in tennis or racquetball, you will know how much effort it takes. A friend of mine had trouble setting the burglar alarm in her new house because the red light in the new system meant "activated" whereas in the previous house, the red light meant "off." That difficulty reflected interference, and it would have bothered her even if she were 18.

You may be wondering if aging makes change more difficult because habits become more ingrained. Although common sense tells us that the answer should be yes, there are no studies that show whether habits you have had for forty years are harder to change than those you have had for five.

RESEARCH EVIDENCE

In a study of interference, one group of subjects studied six lists containing similar words and was then asked to recall words from the first list only. The second group studied only two lists of similar words and had to recall those from the first list. As you would expect, the first group had more trouble remembering the words. Increases in interference from successive lists have been equivalent for older and younger subjects.

In another study, participants were asked to recall words (previously memorized) after they completed a number of activities such as sorting a deck of cards or doing a page of arithmetic problems. As the number of intervening tasks increased, correct recall decreased. The size of the decrease was the same for both age groups.

Forgetting Rates

The rate of forgetting something that is already well-learned does not change with age. Since it may take longer for you to learn when you are older, it is gratifying to know that your hard work and persistence will pay off. Once you have learned a new hobby, a new song, or a new skill, you will retain it for as long as you could when you were young.

FORGETTING RATES IN DAILY LIFE

I am not suggesting, by any means, that you will not forget things. Once you have learned something, however, you should not forget it any faster than you did when you were younger. You will not suddenly forget new job procedures or new dance steps, the way around your office building, the way to operate a food processor, or the times of regular meetings, because you have already learned this information well.

RESEARCH EVIDENCE

In a typical study of forgetting rates, older people and college students examine words, presented one at a time. Many words are repeated; the participants are supposed to identify the ones they have seen before. Sometimes a word is presented again after only a few intervening words (GAME, TELEPHONE, PEAR, GAME). Other times there is a long interval between the first and second presentations. When the interval is longer, there are fewer correct identifications. As intervals increase, younger and older subjects show the same decline in number of correct identifications.

Rate of forgetting is also examined by varying the length of time between studying and taking a test. The number of correct answers typically decreases as the time interval between study and test increases. Older people show no greater decrease in correct answers than young people.

Studies of savings in learning also demonstrate that older people do not forget faster than young people. In this research, two groups are given many different word lists to remember. Each list is studied and then recalled. Without the participants' knowledge, the researcher presents some of the lists more than once. For example, the first, fourth, and eighth list might be the same. If no forgetting occurs, a person should be able to recall most of the words on a repeated list because he has reviewed them previously. The savings, indicated by the difference between recall scores on a repeated and a new list of words, is about the same in both age groups studied.

Search

Whenever you try to remember something, you review the contents of your memory, much as you would look over shelves in a library to find a book or search a cluttered drawer for a utensil. A tip-of-the-tongue experience occurs when your search process gets close to the word or name you want but cannot "locate" it. Although you may search more slowly as you get older, the techniques you use are the same as those used by younger people.

Don't confuse the *technique* of searching with the *results* of searching. Suppose that you and your son are trying to think of the location of a restaurant you both enjoyed a couple of years ago. You may take longer than he will to think of it, or you may eventually remember where the restaurant was fifteen years ago, before it changed locations. Since each of you has different items stored in memory, you will come up with different answers, but you will conduct your mental search in the same way.

SEARCH IN DAILY LIFE

You probably search your mind for information over one hundred times a day. Sometimes you are aware of searching, as, for example, when you are thinking through related words, definitions, and concepts to find a word for a crossword puzzle. Sometimes the definition and a one-letter cue will bring the word to mind automatically, and you will not be conscious of having searched for it.

You will be more aware of searching when it is not successful. You try to recall the name of a movie star and can only remember that her name begins with a B. You try to remember a joke—it would make the perfect opening for the speech you have to give—but can only recall that it involves a gorilla. Memory diaries recorded by adults of all ages indicate that everyone has these blocking experiences and that there are ways to overcome them.

RESEARCH EVIDENCE

When people are given sets of numbers to study for a short-term memory test, their responses reveal their search techniques. Following a brief time for studying the set, participants are shown one number called a "test digit." Their task is to indicate whether or not the test digit was one of the numbers in the study set by pushing a "yes" or "no" button.

Psychologists have discovered that search is usually serial and exhaustive. If you are presented with a 6-4-9 study set, and a test digit of 3, you examine mentally all three numbers in your mind in order of presentation (serial search). Even if the test digit is 6, you still review all of the study set in your mind, 6-4-9 (exhaustive search). Although older people take longer to push the button, their searches are serial and exhaustive, just like those of younger people.

Some investigators have examined the relationship between aging and search efficiency. *Search efficiency* means that you do not spend very long trying to answer a question when you definitely do not know the answer; but you persist in searching for the answer to a question about something you know.

Two psychologists asked people questions about facts, names, and events from the past. They measured the time devoted to searching before the person either recalled the answer or gave up. Each participant then took a multiple-choice test composed of questions he had not answered the first time. If he recognized the right answer, he did indeed have that information available in memory during the first question session. The efficient searchers were the people who spent more time thinking about answers that they later recognized and spent little time thinking about those they did not recognize. Age did not affect search efficiency.

Explanation for Aspects of Memory That Do Not Change

There are few explanations for why these aspects of memory remain fairly stable throughout life. Psychologists have devoted most of their research efforts to explaining differences between age groups rather than similarities. Nevertheless, some comments about these similarities are possible:

The aspects of memory that do not change include those that are not harmed substantially by slowing (forgetting rates, world knowledge, interference), those that do not require the application of strategic thinking (immediate memory), those that occur almost automatically (immediate memory, searching memory contents), and those that are benefitted substantially by experience accumulated over a lifetime (recalling world knowledge, searching through memory contents).

3

How Memory and Aging Is Studied

David and his wife, Ruth, volunteered for a memory experiment at a nearby university. David is 72 and a college graduate; Ruth, 70, did not finish high school. When they got to the campus the morning of the experiment, they had trouble finding a parking space. As they drove around, they became more and more anxious about being late. The space David finally found was three blocks from the psychology building where they were supposed to go, so they walked as fast as they could. By the time they found the right room, Ruth was short of breath and slightly light-headed, though she didn't want anyone to know. After all, the student volunteers were positively glowing with health. David and Ruth went ahead and took the tests. David knew that his wife had pushed herself too hard, and he worried about her throughout the experiment.

As it turned out, David did much better than Ruth, although neither performed as well as the students. Does this mean that memory declines with age? Did David's education, or that of the students, help them do better? Suppose David and Ruth had been tested in their own apartment on everyday memory skills such as locating household items. Would the test results have been different?

Although volunteers for experiments usually do not have as many difficulties as David and Ruth, their story illustrates the kinds of issues that psychologists must consider when they interpret the results of memory research. Most of what we know about memory and aging is based on laboratory tests rather than on daily experience. As with all research on complex topics, there are limits on scientists' ability to generalize test results to all young or old people.

In order to fully understand the memory changes that accompany aging, you should first know how gerontologists—specialists in the study of aging—have reached their conclusions.

PARTICIPANTS

Two Age Groups Studied

Experimental subjects are usually drawn from two groups: college students and adults between the ages of 60 and 85. The college students tend to be freshmen who participate in the experiments for credit in an introductory psychology class. The older adults, who may have had as few as six or as many as sixteen years of education, are usually volunteers. Occasionally, middle-aged adults are also included. The middle-aged or older adults are recruited from clubs and organizations, from high-rise apartment buildings for the elderly, or with newspaper ads.

Most researchers try to recruit older and younger participants who are similar in characteristics that could affect performance, but even so, the two groups may differ from each other in socioeconomic status, intelligence, health, vocabulary experience, and education.

By recruiting separate participants for each experiment and testing each person once, a study can be completed quickly, using the most up-to-date research methods. Each study becomes an independent check on the memory performance of people in those particular age groups.

Testing the Same Individuals

Another logical way to study memory and aging is to test the same individuals repeatedly as they get older. That way, scientists can observe how individuals are affected by the aging process. For several reasons, this approach is rarely used. One is that people who are tested more than once are likely to score higher on the second, third, or tenth try because of familiarity with the testing procedures rather than any improvement in ability.

Another is that people who know they are going to be tested again sometimes behave differently than they normally would between testing sessions. They may, for example, read books and articles about mental improvement in an attempt to increase their scores.

Another problem is that people who score poorly on the first test may refuse to be tested again. So the investigator ends up with a study of how age affects only those people who did well the first time. Finally, it is difficult and expensive for researchers to keep track of experimental subjects in our highly mobile society.

Mark signed up for a series of memory experiments when he was 30 years old. He was supposed to come back every ten years to be tested again. He didn't think it would be a problem to return because he had a good business in town and felt quite settled. But an even better business opportunity came up in another part of the country, so Mark moved away. He was willing to return for the experiment if the university would pay his way. But two other subjects had also moved away, two could not be located at all, one found the first memory test too boring and refused to return, and one subject died. The experimenter didn't have the money to pay for Mark and the two other out-of-towners to return.

Finding Representative Subjects

There may be a problem related to the kinds of people who are tested—college students and older volunteers. Since college students make up only about half of the young adult population and are probably the most competent memorizers in their age group, the test results may be biased in favor of the young. But the results could also be biased in favor of the old. The older adults who participate in memory studies are the kind of people who are active, curious, healthy enough to volunteer for research, and brave enough to try to find their way around a college campus. In other words, they are the *survivors,* and may be as unrepresentative of their age group as college students are of young people as a whole. In other words, only the "best" of each generation is involved in the research.

It is likely, though not yet proved, that the age differences in performance between the best of the old and the best of the young are equivalent to those that would be obtained when comparing "average" older and younger people. At least there is evidence that those who eagerly volunteer for research (after seeing a description of a study) are not more competent than non-volunteers. When non-volunteers of all ages are paid to induce them to participate, their scores are the same as those of the eager volunteers.

Age Differences or Age Changes?

Because of the usual recruiting procedures, the data actually tell us about *age differences* rather than *age changes.* The results indicate the conditions under which younger and older people differ in performance.

After their results are obtained, gerontologists try to determine why these age differences occur. If the young perform better, is it because memory changes or declines as people get older? Is it because the young people are better educated? Is it because the young students are used to taking tests and the older people are not? Although the last two explanations are plausible, the research findings are often interpreted as a reflection of memory changes that occur with age rather than an indication of some of the other differences between the young and old.

This interpretation—that memory changes occur with age—is supported by other research. The data obtained from studies of intelligence using repeated testing of the same individual (with measures of memory and other abilities) is consistent with the data obtained in single-test experimental studies of memory. Thus, the results of the experimental research are probably an accurate reflection of age changes in memory. However, more memory studies are needed in which the same individuals are tested repeatedly as they age.

THE MEMORY TEST

Once the participants are identified, they are usually asked to come to the psychology building or health center on a university campus. In a typical memory experiment, the subjects are told to study words or word-pairs that are presented on slides or flash cards at a fairly rapid rate (at least one word every ten seconds), and afterwards the participants are asked to write down the words they recall. Sometimes a cue is given to aid in recall.

These controlled learning and testing conditions allow scientists to learn more about the ways people use their memory. For example, after a person writes down the words he remembers, the investigator can examine whether or not related words are grouped together. He can also see which cues are most helpful for improving recall.

The data obtained are then averaged for younger or older groups. Individual differences in abilities, often larger for older people, are usually not reported, although they can be dramatic. Since most older people have been away from school and tests for some time, a simple practice task may increase their performance and thereby help reduce age differences. Within both age groups, those people with more education and larger vocabularies tend to score higher than those who have less education and smaller vocabularies.

PROBLEMS IN INTERPRETING THE RESULTS

Lack of Familiarity with Testing Conditions

The older group may be at a disadvantage in memory experiments, not because of their age but because the learning materials, the types of tasks, and the campus setting are not familiar to them. College students are often tested with abstract materials, often have to memorize lists, and certainly feel at home on the campus.

Psychologists have tried to increase the motivation of the older participants to succeed by paying money for high scores or by changing the task requirements (for example, by using grocery lists rather than word lists or letting the individual choose his own words). Monetary rewards do not alter age differences, of course, but one study showed that the older adults actually performed better than college students in a study that included words such as "poultice," "derby," and "pinafore," which were better matched to their generation's vocabulary.

Tests Do Not Assess Everyday Memory

About 85 percent of the studies on aging and memory focus on short-term or long-term memory for lists of words or paired words. There is a serious question about how applicable these tests are to daily life. In the past few years, psychologists have begun to investigate everyday or practical memory.

One investigator tested memory-in-action by watching people maneuver through familiar or unfamiliar supermarkets to get their groceries. She also compared people trying to locate buildings in a familiar city or a new city. She found that where the setting was familiar, there were fewer differences between the old and the young groups.

In my research, I have found that older adults' performance is nearly equal to that of the young in recalling their grocery list, remembering to send a postcard to my office, listing the furniture in their living room, and recalling information about a friend. I am presently examining age differences on everyday tasks such as dialing phone numbers after looking them up, and on nonpractical laboratory tasks such as repeating a series of numbers given verbally by an experimenter.

Recently, other researchers have studied people's recall of television programs, conversations, and daily activities. But it is too soon to draw substantive conclusions. We can't tell yet whether new experiments will demonstrate the same age-related differences that are found in laboratory studies.

4

Memory and
Self-Concept

AGING AND SELF-CONCEPT

Your attitude toward memory changes is as important as the changes themselves. Some people continue to learn as they get older. They continue to use their intellectual ability to its maximum potential, never allowing themselves to use aging as an excuse for mental laziness. Others give up learning anything new and don't try mentally challenging activities because they say that their "aging mind" will not perform.

Beverly is a highly intelligent, well-educated woman in her mid-forties. She teaches English and speaks fluent French, which she learned in college. Recently, she decided to take a Spanish class because she lives in Florida, and many of her friends and neighbors speak Spanish. When students are chatting before the class begins, Beverly likes to announce, for the benefit of anyone who's listening, that her "poor old brain" just cannot remember the verb forms. "At my age," she says, "I'll never master this stuff. I memorize the words one night, and when I do the practice exercises later, I have to study them all over again."

Beverly thinks her brain is deteriorating. But it would be more realistic to attribute her memory problems to a low memory self-concept rather than to age-related mental decline. After all, she can easily rattle off her four children's lengthy lesson, school, and sports schedules (which change each semester), she recalls the names of the students she teaches, she cooks without referring to a cookbook, and she coordinates volunteers for her church. In spite of these obvious indications of memory skill, Beverly feels lost when faced with a task that requires systematic, deliberate memory effort. She has accepted one of society's attitudes toward aging and has lost confidence in her ability to memorize.

Negative stereotypes regarding aging are a primary reason that middle-aged and older people have low self-confidence about their mental abilities. Think for a minute about the images of aging that Beverly—and all of us—are exposed to regularly. On TV there is a 65-year-old woman who is afraid to leave her house because she thinks she will get lost ("Cagney and Lacey"); there is a grandfather still living as if he were in the middle of World War II ("Soap"); a female bailiff on "Night Court" makes one self-deprecating comment after another about her age.

A slogan on a milk carton is accompanied by a picture of a smiling young girl dancing next to a frowning, bearded old man who is leaning on a cane. Advertisements for health aids use older models, but apparently only the young buy cosmetics, soft drinks, and stylish clothes.

Our humor is replete with jokes that remind us that there must be a connection between mental deterioration and aging. I heard one comedian quip, "I'm told that your memory fails when you get older. I'd tell you how old I am but I can't remember!" Jack Benny was not alone in proclaiming himself to be 39 forever. Many of us fudge when we give our age because we assume that anyone who knows the truth will underestimate our capabilities.

In the 1984 presidential campaign, when President Reagan stammered during the first debate with Walter Mondale, his mistakes were immediately translated into an age issue. Many people began to say that a 73-year-old man cannot function as president, merely by virtue of age.

These portrayals are changing, and competent older people are gradually beginning to appear in advertisements and on TV shows. We sometimes hear the catchphrase, "I'm not getting older, I'm getting better!" But the dominant view still emphasizes disability. As a result, many people devalue their abilities as they age and believe that significant memory decline is a normal part of aging.

Even if you don't really believe it, this prevalent negative view can influence your thinking. You may put yourself in the shoes of those you see in the media and begin to feel what they are feeling. In retirement communities, many healthy, competent individuals identify with the few who have diseases such as Alzheimer's, or brain injuries that lead to cognitive difficulties, and say to themselves, "Will I be next?"

Many older people actually accept the myth of severe memory decline as much as, or more so, than younger people. When today's older generation was young, it was commonly believed that "senility" was inevitable. Years ago, if a physician examined an older person who was disoriented or having memory problems, he would more than likely tell the family that Mom or Dad was senile and that there was not much anyone could do about it. Although we now know that such an assumption is unwarranted, it is difficult to throw off years of false beliefs.

When memory failures occur, no matter what the reason, they are usually attributed to aging if the person who makes the mistakes is older. If a young person makes the error, we say it was caused by memory overload ("I have too many things to think about right now"), failure to use appropriate memory aids ("I didn't write it down"), or health problems ("I'm recovering from the flu").

If you believe in the stereotype, even unconsciously, you have set up a barrier for yourself. The barrier is a low memory self-concept, meaning that you don't have confidence in your memory ability. This lack of self-confidence can prevent you from maintaining or improving your memory.

CONSEQUENCES OF A NEGATIVE SELF-CONCEPT

Lack of self-confidence undermines your memory ability in four ways:

It increases anxiety or depression about memory losses, real or imagined.

It leads you to use an unrealistic yardstick to evaluate your own abilities.

It results in reduced memory effort.

It discourages you from seeking intellectual stimulation.

Anxiety

People who have a low self-concept about their memory sometimes worry so excessively about their ability that they become anxious or depressed. Even though these are normal feelings when one is confronted with a real loss, such as a death in the family or a severe illness, it is counterproductive to worry obsessively over losses that may never occur. Such fear is most common in persons who truly believe the negative portrayals about aging.

Whenever I go to a meeting or party with a group of middle-aged or older people, I am aware of their fears. As soon as they find out that my field is memory and aging, I am barraged with questions: "What does it mean when I can't find my glasses—is this a sign that I'm senile?" "I worry because I used to remember names, but they don't stick in my mind anymore." "It takes me so long to recall the figures I use in my business—what's wrong with me?"

Unfortunately, anxiety based on potential, but not actual, memory dysfunction can cause the very problem you fear: you *will* lose some of your memory ability because anxiety interferes dramatically with effective remembering. A case in point is Amelia, whom I met several years ago when I taught a memory training class in a high-rise apartment building populated mainly by widows. These women wanted very much to remember the names of *all* their fellow residents. Amelia was particularly worried about her ability to remember names and was afraid to introduce anyone. She was self-conscious and apprehensive whenever new people were around her because her anxiety about introducing people prevented her from recalling even the names of her most cherished friends! When I trained her to relax before making an introduction, she became more successful.

Anxiety undermines memory at any age. Young people who have severe "test anxiety" because they are afraid of forgetting everything they studied have difficulty achieving high grades.

Unrealistic Expectations

Even if you don't become overly anxious or depressed about potential memory loss, your self-concept may undergo a subtle and gradual erosion if you make unrealistic demands on yourself. You are expecting too much of yourself if you don't take extra time to study something you want to learn. You are being unrealistic if you think that you should be able to concentrate on reading with the television blaring in the next room. When you cannot learn as quickly as you used to and cannot concentrate as well, you need to recognize that you may be experiencing normal age-related changes, instead of thinking that your mind or memory is deteriorating.

Think back to Beverly and her Spanish lessons for a minute. In some ways she's making even greater demands on herself now than she did in college. After all, she was a full-time student then, with no responsibilities other than preparing for class. She studied in the quietest of libraries, and she was motivated by regular tests and grades that affected her academic record and, ultimately, her career. Now that she's studying Spanish "for fun," she attempts to learn the verb forms at the kitchen table while she's waiting for the peas to cook. She memorizes vocabulary in the orthodontist's office while her son gets his braces checked, or in front of the TV set so she can be "close" to the family. Under such conditions, it's not surprising that it might be hard to concentrate and remember. Yet Beverly thinks her memory is failing.

The worst thing about a low self-concept is that it leads you to emphasize your failures. You are likely to jump on every minute memory mistake as "proof" of your failing mind: "I forgot where I put my keys last night and it took me twenty minutes to find them this morning. Maybe I have Alzheimer's." Every forgotten name, missed appointment, or neglected chore is seen as a frightening symptom of senility and an indication that "it's all downhill from here." You "forget" that your memory never did function perfectly all the time.

With a negative self-concept, you fail to notice the number of memory successes you have day after day. If you note every minor failure (almost with glee), but none of the successes, confidence spirals downward.

Lack of Effort

Whether or not you are experiencing real memory problems, lowered self-confidence can lead you to act in ways that indeed weaken your existing memory skills. You may give up too easily on a memory task that you could have accomplished if you had persisted. You may not ask anyone for help because you are certain that you cannot improve. You may not try to learn new memory techniques because you presume that the effort will be wasted. This behavior is self-defeating because, like anxiety and depression, it eventually results in less memory ability and even lower self-confidence. It's a vicious circle.

Michael, a salesman, was transferred to San Francisco at the age of 48. His assignment was to promote a new product and establish a network of clients. If he didn't make the transfer he would lose his job, because the product he had been selling successfully for fifteen years was being phased out. Michael was apprehensive. He had a large amount of technical information to learn about the new product, he had facts and figures to memorize about potential client companies, and he had to learn his way around a new city. He felt that he would never be able to master all of it. He expressed his fear by saying repeatedly, "These old memory cells need a fresh battery and I don't know where to get one."

What happened was predictable. In the first two weeks Michael became frustrated by his inability to learn the product and client information. He convinced himself to quit his job by the end of three weeks because he was "too old to make such changes." If he had been more patient, he could have approached the task systematically, using memory strategies to learn two product facts and two client facts each day. In that way he could have learned almost everything he needed to know for the job by the end of the month, and he could have relied on maps for getting around the city. His success would have been exhilarating and it would have further improved his self-concept. Instead, he tried to remember everything all at once using no memory strategies, got frustrated very quickly, and quit trying. Feeling more insecure than ever, he took a reduction in pay to work for a competitor in his old city.

When you give up in the face of situations that require memory effort, your failure further reduces your self-concept. You believe even more strongly that you won't succeed, no matter what you do.

Lack of Challenge

When you have a low self-concept about your mental ability, you are very likely to create a world around you that does not require you to think very much. You reduce intellectual challenge because of a fear of failure. Bill's story illustrates what can happen when you gradually eliminate intellectual stimulation from your life.

Bill, the stock room supervisor in a large auto parts company, decided at the age of 61 that he wasn't doing his job very well anymore. Memorizing new stock numbers was taking him longer than it used to, and he had to write almost everything else down so he wouldn't forget it. No one else had noticed any change in his job performance. But since he'd never liked his job much anyway, he retired early.

Bill had not planned for his retirement—he had no hobbies and no friends outside the company. So his days were spent watching TV, mostly soap operas, game shows, and old movies. He was bored from time to time, but whenever anyone suggested that he start a hobby or take a class at the local college, he said, "You can't teach an old dog new tricks." Though he read the paper each morning, he made no attempt to remember any of it.

Little by little, Bill became forgetful and stopped paying much attention to what he was doing. He forgot to send out anniversary and birthday cards, though he had always done so before. If someone from the company called and invited him to a party, he forgot to go. He was not suffering from any serious illness and most people thought that he was just getting older. I think that he simply let go.

Because myths about aging are so widely accepted, you may find, as you get older, that people around you suggest that you retreat from difficult tasks. They may recommend a narrowing of life's challenges, even though challenge is how we continue to thrive! In a well-meaning way they will offer to do things for you, "so you won't have to trouble your pretty little head about it." When you leave an environment that requires you to use your mental abilities, it is very easy to sit back and relax because others will not place high memory demands on you.

There can be consequences, however, from allowing yourself to relax. By not challenging your mind, you may no longer be able to meet a challenge when one comes. If a low self-concept leads you to reduce intellectual stimulation, you will induce memory difficulties through disuse of memory faculties.

Anecdotal evidence indicates that even short-term laziness has its consequences.

Harriett, a laboratory administrator, took a six-week vacation to get away from her hectic office. She told me she felt overwhelmed and thought a long rest would be good for her. During her trip she used virtually none of the memory strategies that she had used regularly at work; instead she tried to remember things by repeating them, which is a very weak strategy. When she returned to work, she found it difficult to focus her mind and she had trouble remembering schedules and policies. Her job actually seemed harder than before. Even though she was only 53 years old, Harriett attributed her work problems to "getting older."

I was able to convince Harriet that her difficulty at work had two causes: a recent increase in her professional responsibilities, and a mind that was "out of shape" from the long vacation. With my encouragement, she was able to gradually relearn her complex memory strategy repertoire in only two weeks.

Imagine how difficult it would be to regain skills after letting memory atrophy over a number of years. Allen, a relative of mine, used to say, "The trouble with my memory is that my forgetter gets more exercise than my rememberer." Think of your memory as a muscle that must retain flexibility and strength. Without regular exercise, it won't work well for you when you need it. The message is clear—resting is rusting.

IMPROVING YOUR SELF-CONCEPT

Reject Stereotypes

The first important step in improving your self-concept is to put aside the myths and stop using age as an excuse. If you cannot remember something, think about why the memory failure occurred. Do not say, "I forgot because I'm getting older."

Magazines, newpapers, and TV news programs sometimes feature people over 70 who are still working vigorously, or taking classes, or learning complex new skills. These stories are invaluable for changing society's image of older people. But such stories may also have a subtle effect of making those people seem noteworthy and special. It's important for you to realize that they are not in the minority. Look for new friends among the countless lively, intelligent, and productive "older" people in your community (anyone who is older than you are). They can be your role models.

You can also help yourself by keeping the myths from influencing others. Pass on any positive information you have learned about aging. Tell people that age is not so much the critical factor as health, perceptual ability, mental state, and environment. Now that you know that many aspects of memory and intelligence are maintained throughout a lifetime, don't accept remarks such as, "I'm too old for that." If you see a character in a commercial or television program that reflects the stereotype of inevitable senility, call the station, or write to the company that made the commercial, and say that you find it offensive.

Be Realistic About Your Abilities

A realistic appraisal of your abilities will help you maintain an appropriate level of self-confidence and avoid anxiety or depression.

One way to maintain a balanced view is to make sure that your memory successes get as much attention as your memory failures. You could make a checklist or diary to keep track of them (see Chapter 6); if you do, don't be conservative about claiming success. Each person introduced correctly, each recipe made without the book, or each appointment kept is an example of a memory success.

If the memory mistakes truly outweigh the successes or reflect atypical changes, and you are in good physical and mental health, you should seek a professional evaluation. Otherwise, stop worrying. Most of us have myriads of memory successes each day that go without special notice. And most of us have many minor memory failures that go without special notice—particularly when no one is around to point them out.

Place "blame" correctly. It is easy to misinterpret occasional memory dysfunction or minor mistakes, which can occur for any number of reasons. When you are aware of a memory failure, try to assess the situation objectively. Think back to what you were like when you were younger. Your present abilities may not be significantly different from those of your youth. Didn't you sometimes forget your lunch when you were in high school? Didn't you ever mislay your keys when you were 30? Wasn't it always hard to remember names? Normal age-related changes in ability should be understood rather than feared.

Temporary problems can lead to memory lapses. If a friend or relative has died recently, the emotional impact may affect your memory. You should also not be alarmed if memory difficulties arise after you move, because you will be leaving behind memory clues.

Your memory may be overloaded if you have a great many things to remember at one time. Be aware of the true source and temporary nature of these problems and don't worry that your memory ability is gone forever.

Whatever the conditions responsible for your memory failures, you have options for improving them (except with cases of true senile dementia). Allow yourself a few mistakes, be less sensitive about errors, give yourself time to learn new responsibilities or new surroundings, and teach yourself some memory strategies.

Encourage Intellectual Stimulation

Look for intellectual stimulation, and don't avoid activities that require memory. Encourage your friends to seek out new memory challenges, to join you in learning—about aging, about hobbies, and about the world around you. It takes effort to push yourself out of comfortable ruts of relaxation. When you do it, however, the rewards are new knowledge and a more positive self-image.

There are countless ways you can create enough stimulation to keep your mind alert, though doing so requires planning, motivation, and self-discipline. Volunteer work, political activism, and educational programs at your community college, church or synagogue are all avenues of involvement in every community.

Marvin volunteers one afternoon a week at the information desk at his local hospital. He had asked the director of volunteers to assign him to an easier task because he was afraid, at age 73, that he could never remember how to answer all the visitors' questions. He reluctantly agreed after the director pleaded with him to give it a try. To his surprise and delight, Marvin mastered a great deal of new information, such as the location of the X-ray department, the visiting hours of the maternity ward, the phone number of the hospital chaplain, and much, much more. In addition, he is constantly exposed to new situations and has enjoyed meeting many new people. He is well liked by the other volunteers, the patients, and their families. His self-concept has grown tremendously.

There are also ways to keep alert and mentally active at home. You can work crossword puzzles, anagrams, and acrostics. You can play Monopoly or Trivial Pursuit and plot strategies for winning. You can learn to play bridge or canasta and then work on improving your game. You can discuss television documentaries, educational programs, books, and magazine articles with your friends. While reading books like this one, you can practice memory strategies to remember what you are reading. You can begin a new hobby like gardening, stamp collecting, or chess. You can follow political issues and campaigns and read the congressional record to make sure that your vote is an informed vote. Many older people stimulate their memory for past events by writing a personal history for their children and grandchildren. The point is that you can put memory demands on *yourself*, even when you are in situations that require you to remember very little.

Increase Memory Success

Chances are, if you are reading this book you are either worried about your memory or eager to improve it. In either case, you can improve your memory self-concept by increasing your overall success rate. The best way to do this is to practice and use memory strategies, adding one at a time to your repertoire until you feel more confident about your ability to remember. You must learn to choose when and how to apply memory effort so that your application of strategies will lead consistently to increased memory success.

Maintain a Positive Outlook

There are many benefits to be gained from a positive memory self-concept, in spite of temporary setbacks. You will have less fear and anxiety about situations in which memorizing is needed—with less anxiety you are more likely to remember. You will be more likely to persist in trying to learn something new—if you persist, you are more likely to remember. You will be more likely to approach rather than avoid situations that involve learning—with continued practice, your ability to learn and remember will improve.

Instead of embracing a "gloom and doom" philosophy that

emphasizes age declines wherever they can be found, embrace a "go and do" philosophy that emphasizes positive means to maintain and improve your memory, knowing that you can overcome temporary setbacks. When a child falls off a bicycle we usually say, "Get back up and try again. That's the only way you'll learn." That's also the only way you'll keep your memory ability. Keep using it, and don't believe that it has to deteriorate. It doesn't.

5

Memory and Health

George, a middle-aged business man, spent several anxious months worrying about his memory. He noticed that he had trouble remembering what his colleagues said during meetings, and he couldn't remember the various family responsibilities his wife discussed with him at breakfast. He couldn't remember the story line of TV shows he watched nor the events described on the evening news.

George was afraid to ask anyone about his problem; he thought he was developing Alzheimer's disease. It was his wife who began to suspect that George had a hearing loss. After he got a hearing aid, his memory returned to normal.

Because Alzheimer's disease has received so much publicity recently, it is often the first—and only—explanation that occurs to

63

people who notice some type of memory loss in themselves or in a family member. For many of us, the most fearsome aspect of growing old is the possibility of becoming senile. We dread losing our minds. We are terrified that our families may have to deplete their physical, emotional, and financial resources caring for us when we are too mentally unresponsive to even appreciate the sacrifice.

Fortunately, very few of us will ever have to deal with the profound mental changes caused by Alzheimer's disease. Only about 6 percent of all people over 60 are so afflicted. A higher percentage of people living into their eighties and nineties develop severe and permanent thinking problems, but even among this age group, about 80 percent remain free of serious memory loss.

On the other hand, all of us make memory mistakes when we have temporary health problems, such as an uncorrected hearing loss or a bout of depression. Even a minor illness, such as a cold, can make it harder to remember at any age, and memory failures can be compounded by medications. Memory lapses caused by poor health may occur more frequently as you grow older, not because your mind is weaker but simply because you are more likely to have health problems.

If you or someone in your family has been having memory problems lately, I hope you will not jump to the conclusion that Alzheimer's is responsible, but instead think about the variety of other causes discussed in this chapter and ask your doctor for help.

DEMENTIA

Senility is the word most commonly used to refer to profound and progressive deterioration of mental ability. Dementia is a more appropriate term, however, because *senile* is defined as "relating to old age." One need not be old to have dementia, which is usually caused by Alzheimer's disease or extensive stroke damage. It can be associated with neurological disorders such as Creutzfeldt-Jakob's, Pick's, Huntington's, and Parkinson's diseases, and long-term alcoholism. Temporary memory problems that look like dementia can also be caused by a whole host of illnesses for which there are medical treatments.

Alzheimer's Disease

THE DISEASE

Although interest in Alzheimer's disease has increased dramatically in the last ten years, the condition was first described in 1907 by Alois Alzheimer, a German physician. For many years, doctors believed that this disease, then called "pre-senile dementia," was the cause of dementia only in relatively young people, those not yet in their sixties or seventies. Dementia in the elderly was not attributed to Alzheimer's disease. Instead, it was viewed as an inevitable result of arteriosclerosis, or hardening of the arteries, a condition in which blood flow to the brain is reduced or blocked.

Scientists using sophisticated technology for scanning and examining the brain have recently discovered, however, that the brain cell malfunctions and chemical changes characteristic of Alzheimer's occur in most cases of dementia, no matter what the age of the victim. Alzheimer's disease is now called SDAT, or senile dementia of the Alzheimer's type, and scientists recognize that it is distinct from normal aging and from other forms of dementia. They now recognize that approximately 70 percent of the cases of dementia are due to Alzheimer's either by itself or in combination with dementia caused by other illnesses.

The recognition that senile dementia is not a natural part of the aging process is one reason for the recent interest in Alzheimer's. It has become a serious health concern because a higher proportion of the population is living to advanced old age. As the population ages, the social and financial costs of the disease increase.

Alzheimer's is a great unsolved puzzle—scientists don't know what causes it, they have no exact means to diagnose it in the living patient, and they don't know how to cure it. Many potential causes are being explored, including genetic disorders (if you have a family member with this condition, you have a higher probability of getting it when you are older), slow viruses that attack the brain, failure of the body's immune system, breakdowns in nerve cells that use acetylcholine (a brain chemical related to mental abilities), and excess aluminum in the brain that damages nerve cells.

SYMPTOMS

Memory loss is the most well-known symptom of Alzheimer's. The individual forgets, forgets that he forgets, and doesn't care. Self-awareness and concern about forgetting are usually present only in the early stages of the disease.

In addition to memory loss, family members may see other early signs. These include apathy, weakening of inhibitions, and moodiness. The victim's grooming habits may deteriorate. It may become impossible for him to learn even simple information, such as a name. Personality characteristics such as dependency or assertiveness may become exaggerated. Or the ill person may develop traits opposite to those he once had, such as becoming voluble when he used to be quiet. If he is working, he will find it difficult or impossible to carry out responsibilities that require concentration and persistence.

As the disease progresses, attention and concentration problems become more serious. Not only does the individual fail to remember anything new, but he also may forget well-learned information, such as how to find his way around the city where he lives. He may become disoriented and show such poor judgment that it is not safe to leave him alone.

It is not hard to understand why Alzheimer's is frequently accompanied by depression, anxiety, or paranoia. Victims become depressed because they can no longer do the simple things they want to do. They have intense anxiety reactions because they don't grasp who they are or how they got to a specific place, and they may think that misplaced possessions have been stolen.

As it progresses, Alzheimer's affects the body as well as the mind. The victim may lose bladder and bowel control and have trouble speaking or walking. Eventually, the patient may not recognize his family, and his family may not recognize him because of the dramatic changes in personality, thinking ability, and motor skill.

PROGNOSIS

Although there are variations in the course of the disease, a progressive deterioration in the ability to function on a day-to-day basis is characteristic. The individual usually lives for about three to ten years after diagnosis.

There is no way, at present, to halt the progression of Alzheimer's. Some drugs have been found to improve the mental functioning of some patients, but so far there is no strong experimental evidence for the effectiveness of any drug.

Multi-Infarct Dementia

THE DISEASE

When brain damage occurs because of cerebrovascular accidents—strokes—it can lead to multi-infarct dementia. A stroke occurs when the blood supply to an area of the brain becomes blocked or there is bleeding in the brain. When the blood supply (carrying oxygen and essential nutrients) is reduced, areas of the brain no longer function well, resulting in mental or physical problems. This form of dementia is associated with cardiovascular disease, particularly arteriosclerosis and high blood pressure.

SYMPTOMS

The common symptoms of stroke are confusion, slurred speech, or weakness in some part of the body. If the stroke is relatively minor, the patient may recover his mental abilities, speech, and strength. But when repeated strokes occur, recovery becomes more and more limited. Stroke is the underlying cause of approximately 20 percent of all dementia cases. Of course, the mental problems of people with Alzheimer's may be compounded by brain damage due to stroke.

PROGNOSIS

Although brain damage from stroke cannot usually be reversed, medical intervention using drugs and therapy can reduce the chances of further stroke damage by improving the patient's cardiovascular system. Speech and physical therapy may help restore normal function.

Distinguishing Between Multi-Infarct Dementia and Alzheimer's

Although these conditions can be distinguished from each other with a brain biopsy, the primary method for differentiating between them is to study the person's behavior and medical history. The doctor will look for indications of arteriosclerosis or cardiovascular problems such as high blood pressure, heart disease, minor strokes, or a history of blackouts.

The symptoms provide some clues. Alzheimer's causes gradual and progressive deterioration of mental ability, whereas multi-infarct dementia is more likely to begin suddenly and produce episodes of disorientation, memory loss, and motor difficulties, followed by periods of complete lucidity. Motor problems, dizziness, headaches, and fatigue are also more common in the early stages of this disorder than in Alzheimer's. Multi-infarct dementia often has less impact on mood and motivation than does Alzheimer's, though the victim may, understandably, become depressed or anxious about his condition.

Other Diseases That Cause Dementia

Creutzfeldt-Jakob's disease, caused by a virus, leads rapidly to severe dementia. Huntington's disease is an inherited disorder characterized by mental failure, temperamental behavior, and abnormal movements. Like Alzheimer's, this disease progresses slowly. Pick's disease is similar to Alzheimer's though personality changes may be more striking in the early stages than memory loss. Dementia may occur in the later stages of Parkinson's disease.

These disorders can usually be distinguished from Alzheimer's with a thorough physical and psychological examination, including a brain scan. The physician may diagnose the disease by noting physical symptoms rather than memory problems, especially with Huntington's and Parkinson's diseases.

OTHER PHYSICAL CONDITIONS

Problems in the Brain

There are other health problems, many of which can be treated, that can be mistaken for Alzheimer's disease because the symptoms are similar. In fact, treatable illnesses account for about 10 to 15 percent of the dementia cases. Among these are encephalitis, meningitis, and syphilis—infections that attack the brain and cause intellectual deterioration or emotional disturbances.

Structural brain changes such as a brain tumor, hydrocephalus (excess fluid in the brain), or subdural hematoma (accumulation of blood in the brain) can also result in concentration problems, memory lapses, and physical or mental slowness. Brain scans can often be used to detect these structural problems.

Metabolic and Nutritional Problems

Chemical imbalances in the body can cause mood disturbances, confusion, apathy, thinking problems, or disoriented behavior. Imbalances can be due to malfunctions of glands (like the thyroid gland) or major organs (such as the kidney), severe vitamin or mineral deficiencies or excesses (for instance, vitamin B12 deficiencies, anemia, or elevated calcium levels), or hypoglycemia (low blood sugar). These conditions can be discovered with a thorough physical examination.

Congestive Heart Failure

Congestive heart failure can lead to impaired mental performance because of reduced blood and oxygen flow to the brain. This is particularly true for people already experiencing some memory failures.

What You Can Do

You should see your doctor immediately if any of the above symptoms arise. If you have any of these physical conditions, you have probably noticed many symptoms besides your memory problems. In the majority of cases, memory problems, disorientation, or personality disturbances disappear completely after treatment, although, unfortunately, some diseases progress quite far before treatment is sought.

CHRONIC ILLNESS

Direct Impact

A weak or inefficient cardiovascular system is an example of a chronic illness that can affect your memory. The most serious consequence of cardiovascular disease, as noted previously, is stroke. But even without a stroke, cardiovascular disease can impair the intellect. Serious cardiovascular difficulties reduce the flow of blood and oxygen to the brain so that it cannot function efficiently. Mental skills deteriorate if the condition persists.

Older adults with a healthy cardiovascular system show greater blood flow to the brain and less slowing of brain activity than adults with cardiovascular disease. In a study of the relationship between health and mental ability, the investigator asked experienced pilots and air traffic controllers to perform some simple timed tasks. None of these men was acutely ill, but some had a history of cardiovascular problems. Performance declined as the degree of cardiovascular disease increased.

What You Can Do

To maintain a healthy cardiovascular system, you need to maintain reasonably low blood pressure. Try to exercise regularly and reduce the amount of stress in your life. Have regular checkups for your heart and blood pressure, remember to take blood pressure medication if it is prescribed, and always consult your physician before beginning an exercise program.

In a recent study of the effects of exercise on mental performance, investigators randomly placed volunteers, who ranged from 55 to 70 years old, into an aerobic exercise group, an easy calisthenics group, and a no-exercise control group. Most of the volunteers were in poor-to-fair physical condition at the beginning of the program.

Brisk walking three times a week was the main exercise for the aerobics group. Members of this group began with three to five minute exercise periods and worked their way up to forty-five to fifty minute periods at the end of four months. The calisthenics performed by the second group were designed to improve general physical fitness but were not sufficiently vigorous to improve the body's use of oxygen.

The three groups were similar in terms of oxygen consumption, physical fitness, memory, and mental dexterity before they began exercising. At the end of the program, both exercise groups improved their general level of physical fitness, but the oxygen consumption of the people in the aerobics group was substantially higher than that of the other exercise group. Over the four month period, the mean scores for the aerobics group improved in five out of seven tests for memory and mental dexterity; the other two groups scored higher on only one test each.

Although mental difficulties are associated primarily with severe cases of cardiovascular disease, I would recommend preventive exercise for anyone who is able. Generally speaking, exercise that results in a significant rise in your heart rate (up to 100 or 120 beats per minute for most people) for at least twenty minutes is best for your cardiovascular system. Ideally, you should have a twenty minute workout at least three times a week. The best exercises are brisk walking, swimming, bicycle riding, and running. Any new exercise program should be started very slowly and only under the supervision of your physician.

Indirect Impact

Chronic conditions that cause pain and reduce mobility, such as arthritis, osteoporosis, or heart disease, can have an indirect impact on memory ability because they limit opportunities for intellectual stimulation. If you have any of these problems, you may have dropped out of the social, professional, and civic activites that kept you in touch with the world and required you to use your memory.

If you do not remain active mentally, some of your mental skills will suffer. You may also become so preoccupied with worrying about your condition that you cannot concentrate on things that need to be remembered.

Julia was on the board of the local chapter of the American Association of Retired Persons for several years. She organized meetings, kept track of relevant legislation, and knew the names of many members. Then, as her arthritis got progressively worse, she began to have trouble getting out and eventually stopped going to meetings. She thought of herself as an active member, but actually participated very little. After several years at home, her memory deteriorated.

What You Can Do

If you suffer from a chronic illness, you need to be careful about maintaining your mental skill. Try to avoid becoming preoccupied with your illness, because you may become less attentive to your surroundings. If you find it too taxing to be active socially, try to bring intellectual stimulation into your home with books, television study courses, or mental games such as crossword puzzles or Scrabble. Invite friends over regularly and discuss current events with them.

If at all possible, keep active in causes that interest you. Don't be embarrassed to ask for rides to meetings or events if you no longer drive. Invite clubs or organizations to meet at *your* house, and don't worry if you can't prepare refreshments. Let someone else do that. You still have ideas to contribute. Make an effort to keep your mind alert.

TEMPORARY ILLNESS

Effects of Minor Illness

Colds, flu, and short-term infections such as an ear infection or bronchitis, can sap your mental as well as your physical energy.

When you are ill, it is difficult to put forth effort for anything, and that includes remembering. Your thinking is sometimes fuzzy, and you feel too tired to concentrate. Unfortunately, older people have health problems more frequently than young people.

Poor health has a powerful effect on memory ability at any age. My 6-year-old daughter, who has been reading for about a year, cannot remember the simplest of words when she is ill. She simply hasn't the energy to concentrate and push herself to succeed.

Recently, I went to see the doctor because I thought I had the flu. I had just moved to a new city and was making my first visit to this particular doctor. I had, however, visited a building only two blocks away from the doctor's office, so I thought I was familiar with the neighborhood. Even so, I lost my way. Feeling ill, and unable to regroup my thoughts, I turned the wrong way at least three times before I got there. Then it took me twenty-five minutes to fill out a simple one-page medical history because I couldn't think.

What You Can Do

The lesson here is that if you experience memory difficulties during times of illness, you should first assume that the illness is the cause. It's not that your memory is going, going, gone, it's just that an illness is draining away the energy that you would normally devote to remembering. Therefore, do not expect to perform well when you have a cold and don't try to learn new skills when you are feeling under the weather.

You can try to avoid colds and other temporary illnesses somewhat by maintaining good health habits. Make sure that you get enough sleep, and rest when you feel tired. Get regular exercise, even if it just involves walking around the block or doing mild calisthenics in your home. Eat a balanced diet of dairy products, fruits and vegetables, meats (including poultry, fish, and beans), and whole grains.

DRUGS AND MEMORY

Many medications can exacerbate any memory difficulties you might have when you are ill. Drugs can cause confusion, a slowing of behavior, problems in concentration and attention, and mood swings. These drug effects reduce your ability to think clearly and to remember, and they can also lead to a mistaken diagnosis of dementia. The main and most obvious sign of a drug reaction is that your problems develop rapidly (except in the case of alcoholic dementia, which develops after years of alcohol abuse).

Effects Change with Age

Drugs can affect memory at any age, although changes in body chemistry that are a normal part of aging may increase your sensitivity to prescription drugs, over-the-counter medicines, alcohol, caffeine, or tobacco. Older people may need reduced dosages to prevent adverse drug reactions.

Problems with Drug Combinations

You must be especially alert to drug effects if you take more than one medication. It is not unusual in these days of the specialty physician for a person to be taking three drugs prescribed by three different physicians, who have not discussed the case.

Some drug combinations can make you physically ill; others can cause disorientation, poor judgment, or memory loss. These reactions can occur not only with two or more prescription drugs but also with a combination of prescription and over-the-counter drugs. Failure to follow the doctor's instructions for taking medicine can result in dangerous side effects that influence memory and thinking ability.

Specific Drugs

Tranquilizers such as Valium or Lithium can lead to slowing and lack of alertness. Alcohol, in combination with prescribed or over-the-counter medicines, causes similar symptoms. Antidepressant drugs often have strong effects on the cholinergic system in the brain (cholinergic activity is related to memory ability), and may lead to memory failures. Bromides used for anxiety (and present in some over-the-counter medicines) can be dangerous because they can lead to delirium or mental disorder.

Sleeping pills and sedatives are notorious for their effects on mental performance, especially in the elderly. If you do not get as much sleep as you used to, you may be experiencing a normal, age-related change in your sleep pattern. Generally speaking, you will get less deep sleep as you get older. You may wake up more frequently at night or get up very early in the morning. Don't count on sleeping pills to help reestablish the sleep patterns of younger years. The pills can actually interfere with deep sleep and can remain in your system during the day, causing sluggishness and memory problems.

What You Can Do

Never underestimate the power of a drug. Always ask your physician about the possible side effects of any drugs that are prescribed for you. Keep a list of the names and dosages of all the drugs you take, including over-the-counter medications, and show it to any doctor who treats you. This will help him or her to prescribe medications that will have minimal side effects for you. Do not take a new over-the-counter preparation without checking with your doctor first.

Make sure that you have understood the directions for taking the medicine before you leave the pharmacy. If you have vision problems, ask your pharmacist to make labels with large type or to use bottles of different shapes, sizes, and colors for different medications. Also, never take drugs prescribed for someone else, even if you have the same symptoms.

Monitor yourself very carefully for at least a week when you begin taking a new medication or when the dosage is changed. Some side effects occur only after the medicine has accumulated in your body for several days. Notice any behavior changes. Are you more irritable now? Can you concentrate as well as you usually do? Are you feeling dizzy? Is it difficult to focus your eyes? Are you forgetting more? If you have these types of changes, find out first if they could be drug induced by checking with your doctor or pharmacist.

PERCEPTUAL DEFICITS

You should expect some decline in your vision and hearing as you grow older. This is perfectly normal and may begin as young as your early forties. Changes may be as subtle as a slight decrease in your ability to understand high-pitched voices or to read the newspaper while holding it in its normal position. For some people these changes may eventually be as dramatic as an inability to hear anything clearly without a hearing aid or to read without a magnifying glass. Moderate declines in touch, taste, and smell sensitivity also occur with age.

Perceptual deficits have a direct impact on memory. If you don't hear something clearly, you won't remember it correctly. You may remember a man's name as John Gordon when he was actually introduced as John Goodenauer. If you can't read a sign easily, you can't remember what it says. It is more difficult to pay attention and retain something if it is fuzzy or unclear.

People with vision and hearing problems may be unaware of their difficulties and assume that their mistakes are due to poor memory. If you feel as if your memory problems are increasing, ask yourself, Do I have trouble concentrating on a conversation? Do I forget what I've read? Do I have trouble finding things at night when the house is darker? If the answer to any of these is yes, you may have a perceptual problem rather than a memory problem.

Vision

Most people develop presbyopia, a normal decline in close-up vision, beginning around age 40. Presbyopia is the result of loss of flexibility in the eye's focusing mechanism, the lens. With age, the lens becomes less able to change shape, as it once did, to focus clearly on objects that are close to the eye. Reading is more difficult, especially with fine print. Rapid changes in focusing from distant to nearby objects can no longer be done easily. Presbyopia is the main reason why people need reading glasses or bifocals.

About one-third of the older population suffers from poor visual acuity (20/50 or worse). A gradual yellowing of the lens of the eye affects color sensitivity and reduces the amount of light entering the eye. The pupils become smaller, further reducing the amount of available light and making it more difficult to see. At the same time, the eyes become more sensitive to glare. Because the process of dark adaptation slows down, it takes longer for the eyes to adjust to changes in light.

Cataracts are also more common in older people. A cataract is a clouding of the lens, so that light is kept from entering the eye; vision becomes dimmer as the lens gradually becomes more opaque. Vision may be improved by removing the opaque lens surgically and replacing the lost optical power of the eye with glasses, contact lenses, or a surgically implanted intraocular lens.

Hearing

Hearing losses also occur gradually as people get older, but they accelerate in later years. There is a decline in acuity, especially for higher-pitched tones, and some people find it difficult to discriminate between sounds of different pitches. Some older people develop tinnitus, or "ringing in the ears." Interference from distracting noises increases with age. It may be more difficult to carry on a telephone conversation when the television or radio is on.

These changes are due partly to a loss of flexibility in some membranes in the ear and partly to reductions in nerve connections between the ears and the brain. Hearing deficits affect social life because they make it difficult to carry on conversations.

What You Can Do

Since perceptual deficits can lead to memory difficulties, you should be realistic about your problems. Have your eyes and ears checked regularly, and don't be afraid to get glasses or a hearing aid if the doctor recommends it. Some people are reluctant to use corrective devices because of vanity. But your friends will not think less of you for taking the advice of your physician. They are more likely to think less of you if you don't wave to them across a room because you cannot see them. They are more likely to avoid socializing with you if you cannot hear well enough to understand what they have said.

Alter your environment to reduce the likelihood of memory problems related to hearing and vision changes. Make sure that you have a very good light for reading, without glare or shadows. Give your eyes time to adjust when going from a bright room to a dark one and vice versa. If you drive at night, be aware that your eyes will take longer to adjust to changes in light.

If you have difficulty hearing, ask your friends to speak clearly and loudly, and in a low-pitched voice. Ask people to stand directly in front of you when they are speaking so you can use visual cues to ensure that you are understanding correctly. Ask family members to make sure that you are paying attention *before* they tell you something important. You may need to turn off the radio or television while you are using the telephone. A sound magnifier can also be installed on your telephone.

MENTAL HEALTH AND MEMORY

Depression and anxiety can occur at any age, but they are the two most common psychological problems experienced by older adults. Both types of disturbances have an impact on memory, and both can develop as reactions to losses associated with aging: loss of loved ones and friends; loss of status or income; loss of mental ability, hearing, vision, physical vigor, or independence. Multiple losses make adjustment more difficult and are more common for older people than for the young.

Depression

Depression is often called "pseudo-dementia" because its symptoms can be mistaken for those of true dementia. Keith is a patient of mine whose story is typical.

About eight months after his company went bankrupt, Keith's wife insisted that he see their family physician because she thought he had Alzheimer's disease. Keith had difficulty concentrating and lost interest in painting and playing the violin, activities he had once enjoyed. He was often agitated and irritable. His wife complained that he wouldn't eat his favorite meals any more and that he never remembered what she said to him. Keith's physician discovered that he was feeling inadequate because he had made many bad business decisions, and that he felt responsible for his company's losses and for the employees who lost their jobs when the business failed. It took a sensitive physician to recognize depression as the source of Keith's problems and to help him accept the situation.

Anxiety

Anxiety causes similar symptoms. Highly anxious people are agitated and may have trouble sleeping. They may feel fearful, tense, and under stress without knowing the source of those feelings. Anxious people often show signs of excessive sensitivity to people and events, making a "big deal" out of a minor embarrassment or joke. They become so preoccupied with personal tensions that they have trouble maintaining concentration and paying attention.

Effects on Memory

Successful remembering requires attention and concentration, motivation and effort, and the application of memory strategies. If you are highly agitated, you won't be able to pay attention or focus your thoughts on something you need to remember. Even if you try to concentrate, you will have a hard time remembering. Feelings of guilt or excessive worry about minor problems can dominate your thinking and make it almost impossible to recall events you once remembered easily. The slowing down of thinking often associated with depression makes it difficult to apply effective memory strategies.

Temporary memory problems are likely to occur after a divorce or the death of your spouse. Grieving uses a great deal of mental energy.

For months after her husband died, Margaret did little more than try to get through each day. She suffered bouts of depression and did not want to leave the house to visit her family. Her son began to hear from creditors that she was not paying her bills, and the lawyer could not finish the paperwork for the estate because Margaret would not give him the information he requested. She kept saying, "I can't remember." In her grief, Margaret did not want to be bothered to remember anything. Her son realized that her mind couldn't be expected to function well when it was so thoroughly preoccupied with grief, so he helped her complete the legal and financial tasks. It took eight months after her husband's death for Margaret to get back on her feet again, functioning reasonably well.

What You Can Do

When emotional or personal problems overwhelm you, find someone you trust to talk to. You can confide in a good friend or clergyman or seek help from a professional counselor. Many older people tend to see their family physician when they are depressed, using physical complaints as a means of getting some attention for the personal problem. All too often, the "cure" is a pill that may alleviate the patient's physical symptoms but does nothing to resolve his personal crisis.

You need to recognize when your emotional state has affected your thinking ability. If you have experienced losses and have felt anxiety or depression, you can expect temporary memory difficulties. After resolving your personal problems, your memory will return to normal.

RULING OUT ALZHEIMER'S DISEASE

If you or someone in your family has been having memory problems, you are undoubtedly concerned about whether the condition is temporary or permanent. Your greatest fear is Alzheimer's disease. Although the final diagnosis will have to be made by a physician, you can help by evaluating the nature of the memory errors that are occurring.

Types of Memory Problems

Consider the kind of information that is forgotten and the situation in which the forgetting occurs. If new information is forgotten in a new setting, and there are no other problems, you do not need to be especially concerned.

Alice is worried about her father, who has just come for a visit; he cannot recall her work schedule or where she will be on any given day. She should not be surprised. This is new information that he has not tried to memorize, nor is he motivated to remember it. He probably didn't pay close attention when she told him. If her father shows that he can still learn something new when he makes an effort, he probably does not have a serious problem.

She should be worried, though, if he forgets new information that she has repeated many times and that is important for him. If they go shopping, for example, and decide to shop separately for awhile, he should not forget that he came with Alice and needs to go home with her. She should not be alarmed, however, if he forgets exactly where to meet her.

Another cause for concern is forgetting old information in a familiar setting. If your wife has been a file clerk for fifteen years and begins to complain that she is struggling with the alphabet and cannot decide where to file things, she may have the beginnings of a serious memory problem. Well-practiced skills such as filing alphabetically should be retained throughout life. Also, a person should not forget the meanings of simple words, the names of close relatives, or the skills required to do simple arithmetic. Errors in these types of mental activity can be a signal that there is severe and permanent memory loss.

Ask yourself if the problems that concern you are typical or atypical. Perhaps Sam has never been a great bridge partner and has always had trouble remembering the bids. Now you have to remind him twice as often. Still, the errors he makes are just an exaggeration or extension of his usual errors.

But what about Larry, an executive who has never had any trouble remembering his appointments and responsibilities? He's always used a calendar for backup but has rarely consulted it. Now you see him taking his calendar with him everywhere he goes, checking it every thirty minutes and "holding on for dear life" to this written reminder of his duties. In addition, you have noticed many small signs of gradual decline in his job effectiveness. Atypical behavior such as this can be an indication of dementia.

Another symptom of dementia is loss of immediate memory skill, which usually does not decline with age. A person who is not interrupted should be able to look up a zip code or phone number, say it once or twice, and write it down. A person who is paying attention and is not distracted should be able to recall, a few minutes later, what was said during a conversation that has just ended. On the other hand, a person of any age will have trouble picking up the thread of a conversation if he is distracted or interrupted. Think about your situation or that of your friend or relative—is he or she showing immediate recall errors? That may be a signal of profound memory disturbance.

If any of these signs of dementia occur, you should seek a professional evaluation of the person's abilities. If severe memory problems truly exist, the second step in the diagnosis is to determine the cause.

MEDICAL EXAMINATION

Even with the sophisticated medical technology available in the 1980s, the diagnosis of Alzheimer's disease is still primarily one of exclusion. The only certain diagnosis is made with a brain biopsy (usually done during an autopsy). The physician faced with a patient who has severe memory and thinking problems will attempt to rule out all other illnesses or diseases that could cause these problems.

He will take a family history to see if the patient could have an inherited disorder. Brain scans will be ordered to check for internal damage. He will ask the patient to stop taking medications, if possible, to eliminate drugs as the cause. Then he will run laboratory tests to examine the organs and metabolic functioning. He may use psychological tests to assess the presence of emotional disturbances such as depression. Tests of intellect and memory can detect changes that normally do not occur in older people.

When a person shows progressive deterioration of memory, loss of awareness of himself and his environment, or mood disturbances, and a complete physical and psychological examination does not reveal other health problems that could have caused these symptoms, the person will be diagnosed as having Alzheimer's disease. If someone in your family does develop dementia, you will find invaluable practical suggestions for home care and sympathetic guidance for handling your own frustrations as caregiver in *The 36 Hour Day* by Nancy Mace and Peter Rabins.

THE FUTURE

Now that scientists know that senility is not an inevitable part of aging, the challenge is to prevent and cure it. One way to meet the challenge is to educate people about controllable factors, such as high blood pressure, that may lead to memory problems. Another is continued research, now being carried out from many different perspectives, into the causes and treatment of dementia.

In the meantime, if you or anyone in your family show signs of severe memory loss, do not hesitate to get a thorough examination from a physician and a psychologist. Fortunately, the odds are good that you don't have Alzheimer's disease. You may be misinterpreting the severity or nature of your memory problems or they may be due to a treatable condition, in which case memory function can be restored.

6

Memory Awareness and Evaluation

Most of us are not conscious of how we use our memory. Even though we carry out countless memory tasks every day, we usually don't take note of the mental effort we are expending. We are not aware of the methods we use to remember, nor do we know why we forget. Our memory just works or doesn't work, "naturally."

At the age of 66, Rebecca took one of my memory courses. She discovered during class discussions that, like most people, she was rarely aware of the way she used her memory. One time was obvious, however. About a year before, she had registered for an art history course at the university. She was determined to do well, and for her hard work she received an A on the first exam. But she did it at great expense to her personal life because, in order to memorize everything, she "lived, breathed, and slept" art history.

Eventually she dropped the class because it required so much memory effort. Rebecca knew that she could be an "ace" student, but she chose to put her mental effort elsewhere.

Rebecca's awareness of her abilities and limits contrasted with her confusion about current memory problems. She reported in the class that she could never remember to finish her errands or even a letter, and she didn't know why. She thought this was odd because when she had worked part-time three years earlier, she had accomplished tasks on schedule.

As part of the memory course, Rebecca kept a diary for a week, describing situations in which she remembered and forgot. Her problem became obvious to me when I reviewed the diary; when she was at home she let herself get distracted. But when she had someone else motivating her, such as an instructor or employer, she focused on the job at hand and completed the required assignments.

Rebecca was aware of the mental effort she had expended on the art history class, and she was surprised to learn that it was a lack of concentrated effort that prevented her from remembering household responsibilities. Her new awareness made it possible for her to make the necessary changes in her behavior. We worked on ways for her to increase concentration, to avoid distractions, and to remember what she was doing if she was interrupted.

CHOOSING WHAT TO REMEMBER

To increase your own memory awareness you should become aware of what you remember and how you remember it.

You Cannot Remember Everything

Like everyone else, you have limits on the amount of memory power you can muster at any one time. There is no way for you to remember every movie you've seen, every book you've read, every conversation you've heard, every person you've met, everything you've ever done.

If you tried to remember such trivial and irrelevant information from even one day, you would have to expend tremendous effort and you would undoubtedly overload your memory. So it is appropriate that, consciously or unconsciously, you make choices about how to use your memory power.

Recognize When Effort Is Needed

Knowing that it is not possible to remember everything, you probably do what most people do, which is to settle back and see what happens. You probably figure that you will remember what is important. Unfortunately, motivation alone cannot guarantee remembering. Memory failures will certainly occur if you do not consciously apply memory effort when it is needed.

I am not considered to be an absent-minded professor because I am generally well-organized. I remember books and articles I've read, the family social calendar and financial obligations, and many birthdays, addresses, and phone numbers. But my memory is a total failure when I don't use it.

Several years ago I was teaching a memory course at a business near my office. I usually walked there, but one day I had an errand to do so I took the car. Afterwards, totally forgetting about the car, I walked back to my office. About an hour later a student asked me for a paper that I knew was in my briefcase (which was in the car). That should have cued me that I had broken my routine that morning, but it didn't. All I did was make a mental note to get the briefcase later.

Two hours later I decided to get the briefcase and I tried to visualize parking my car on campus, but the image eluded me. *Finally*, I recalled the events of that morning.

What happened? I didn't bother to apply the memory effort to note a change in routine. You see, you can have a terrific memory, but it's of no use unless you make it work for you.

Be Aware of Your Memory Choices

Although you may sometimes need to memorize something because someone else—such as a friend or employer—asks you to, most of the time your memory choices are up to you. Learn to become aware of these choices and make sure they are the best ones for you.

The best memorizers are people who know when and how to remember. They are conscious of the memory choices they make. They focus their attention on retaining particular information and don't pay much attention to other things. By applying their effort and mental energy selectively, they give themselves a greater chance for memory success.

MAXIMIZE YOUR STRENGTHS

To use your memory power as effectively as possible, take on memory tasks that are compatible with your strengths—in other words, tasks that are related to a subject with which you have some familiarity and that can be approached with memory methods that work well for you. Then take into account the time you have available for memorizing.

Ben was looking forward to a trip to France in three months. He knew that he would get more out of the trip if he devoted his spare time to learning something about French history, art, and architecture. But he soon realized that it would be difficult to remember much about architecture or art; he had little background in these areas and all of the terminology was unfamiliar. Moreover, he was not good at visualizing. So he decided to concentrate on history, and found it relatively easy to connect people and events in French history with his general knowledge of the past in Europe and America.

Of course, the more you practice and become skilled at using a variety of memory strategies, the more memory choices you will have opened up to you. You will gain confidence in tackling unfamiliar subjects and you will be able to remember more in less time. But you will still have to make choices.

CHOOSING TO FORGET

Are there areas of your life that you choose to forget because you do not want to apply memory effort to them? A friend of mine, Carol, is terrible at Trivial Pursuit because she chooses to forget movie plots, the details of novels, and the names of actors, actresses, and composers. She enjoys the entertainment at the time and then "lets it go." There's nothing wrong with that. Don't waste energy trying to remember things that are not important to you.

SHARED MEMORY

Over the years, husbands and wives often develop a system for dividing the memory requirements of their shared lives. They provide cues and reminders for each other. This shared mental effort is often sensible, and sometimes necessary.

Richard is a busy executive who doesn't even try to keep track of details in his home life because his wife, Mary, handles that job so well. He remembers business meetings, his investments, and letters he needs to write clients, but he forgets birthdays and social engagements. He doesn't know when the children last saw the dentist, when the service repairman cleaned the furnace, where his aunts and uncles live, or where the good dishes are kept. This man is hopeless at home but highly efficient at the office. His represents a fairly typical memory pattern in that he focuses all his effort in one domain and intentionally lets it relax in others.

CHOOSING HOW TO REMEMBER

After you decide that it is important to expend the effort needed to remember something, you have to decide how you are going to accomplish your goal. Awareness is critical. You need to be aware of the memory techniques you can choose from and the reasons for choosing one over another.

Without this awareness, you will probably unconsciously use a well-practiced but perhaps inappropriate strategy from your repertoire. For example, you may be a visualizer who typically remembers by using mental pictures. If you need to pass on a message to your husband that next week's Great Books discussion is canceled, it will take some thought to use visualization—how can you picture a meeting cancellation?

WHAT ARE YOUR OPTIONS?

As a visualizer, your first reaction is to picture yourself talking to him about it. But that's not going to be terribly effective because the next day when you see him, and think of your image, you may not recall what you were supposed to say.

When you are aware of selecting a strategy, you can choose a technique that will be more likely to lead to success. The point is that awareness allows you to think through alternative methods and choose the best ones for the memory activities you need to do. For remembering the Great Books message, the following strategies are reasonable options.

External (outside your head) strategies:

1. Write him a note.

2. Leave the current "great book" he is reading on the bathroom counter.

Internal (inside your head) strategies:

1. Associate reading a book with reading the morning newspaper. Remind yourself at intervals to mention it at breakfast when you usually discuss the news.

2. Imagine him jumping up and down on the book (canceling it out).

External Strategies Expand Memory Power

The sum total of your memory power includes everything you can remember, both internally and externally. Most people do not think that the word "memory" applies to written notes. They say, "I didn't try to remember it, I wrote it down."

Actually, writing and other external memory strategies are an important extension of your internal memory power. It may not be obvious at first, but the correct application of external methods does require thinking. For instance, with a writing strategy you have to remember to write your reminder down, remember where you have written it (or where the note is placed), and remember to look at the note (or take it with you) when you need it. Thus, this external strategy will not be effective without the use of internal memory, attention, and concentration.

Remember that your goal is memory success and that external strategies improve your chance of accurate recall. If success is guaranteed by using a calendar, then use a calendar. Why not?

Make the Strategy Fit the Task

External and internal strategies vary in effectiveness, depending on the memory task. Think about how *you* remember. Are you making choices that are appropriate for your memory activities?

A datebook or calendar (external strategy) is probably the most practical way to recall appointments, because the information requires constant updating. Many meetings are scheduled far in advance, and there may be subsequent changes in time and place.

An exception is when you are on vacation and have less to remember; then you will probably find it easier to recall your schedule internally by reminding yourself regularly: I'M FISHING WITH LARRY ON FRIDAY AND GOING TO THE CONCERT SUNDAY AFTERNOON.

When it comes to remembering "things to do," most people make lists (external), but you may find it so inconvenient to do this in the middle of a busy day that you retain the information internally, by making a mental list of three errands arranged by first letter—BOMS: stop at bank, stop at office, mail invoices, and get supplies.

You may depend on a map (external strategy) to find your way around a city you are visiting for the first time, especially if you won't need the information for very long. But internal methods, like visualizing the map in your mind, are required when you want to remember the routes for a long time or when you are driving in heavy traffic and can't stop to read the map.

Combining Internal and External Strategies

By combining both types of strategies, you give yourself the greatest memory power possible, and you maintain your internal memory skills by using them regularly. In addition, you will not overload internal memory.

People often say to me, "If I use external cues, won't I be letting my memory muscles deteriorate through lack of use?" That is a possibility if you write everything down the minute it comes to mind and always consult your notes. Although you are probably using more internal memory than you realize, be sure that you use it regularly.

Make a note and remember internally where you put it and what it says.

Write your social plans on a calendar, but rehearse them once or twice a week: TUESDAY I WORK OUT AT THE GYM AT 5:00; WEDNESDAY MORNING IS THE BOARD MEETING; FRIDAY I GO TO THE CLUB.

Keep a list of errands you need to do but test yourself occasionally: ARE THERE ANY ERRANDS I SHOULD DO ON TUESDAY WHILE I'M OUT OF THE OFFICE?

Internal strategies require more mental effort than external ones. You should exercise internal memory when you can. At the same time, you should also use external aids in order to avoid overwhelming your internal memory (which will lead to mistakes).

If you are a social worker with a heavy client load, you could try to remember a week's schedule internally. But your mind would hardly be able to function! Instead, use a calendar (external) when you can, and use internal memory to remember the location of the calendar and the appointments you made when you did not have it with you.

When you are invited to dinner at a neighbor's house, try to internally remember the names of the new people you meet. Later, you can write down the names to be certain that you won't forget them and to let your mind concentrate on something else.

Make a grocery list and keep it in a prominent place; look it over occasionally so that if you make a spontaneous decision to shop without the list, you will remember what was on it.

SELF-EVALUATION

Most people use very few strategies and are quite happily unaware of how they use them. However, becoming aware of what you do to remember is an important first step if you want to improve your memory.

You can increase your memory power most effectively by identifying and building on your existing memory strengths. You can prevent memory failures by identifying when and why they occur. Understanding how you use your memory requires special effort but it is well worth it. The remainder of this chapter suggests ways for you to gain this understanding.

Four Memory Tasks

Your first move toward memory self-awareness should be to ask yourself how you would accomplish particular memory activities. Most of your daily use of memory falls into one of four types of tasks:

Commit new information to memory

Remember and complete errands or actions

Develop habitual behaviors

Recall a past event

We all have a memory repertoire—a set of strategies we use for most of our daily memory tasks. The following exercises help you to identify the memory strategies in your repertoire.

REMEMBER NEW INFORMATION

Suppose, as you read Chapter 3, that you wanted to remember the ways in which memory ability is stable or changes as you age. How would you do it? Would you read the chapter again? take notes? write lists of abilities that change and abilities that are maintained? tell a friend about it? mark the place in the book and go back to it regularly?

Think about which of these memory strategies you would be most likely to use. If you're not sure, memorize this part of Chapter 3, and pay attention to how you do it.

REMEMBER TO DO SOMETHING

Tomorrow you have three errands—visit an acquaintance who is in the hospital, take a suit to the dry cleaners, and buy a birthday present for a friend. How will you remember? How did you remember the last time you had errands like these?

If you don't know, plan three things to do tomorrow, and note how you remember to do them.

REMEMBER HABITUAL ROUTINES

When you leave your house, how do you remember to take your keys, pocketbook, or wallet with you? You may protest that you don't have to "remember," you just do it without thinking. I disagree. Whether or not you are aware of using your memory, a habit does require memory.

If you can't answer the question as to how you remember, create a new routine: take this book with you when you leave the house for the next five days, and pay attention to how you remember.

REMEMBER PAST EVENTS

How would you remember last year's Thanksgiving weekend? Suppose your Aunt Bessie came to see you and is coming again this year. You need to recall what you did with her last year, so this visit can be unique.

If you're not sure how you would go about this memory task, try to recall what you did on Thanksgiving last year. Don't read any further until you have been able to identify what methods you use to remember events from your past.

HOW DID YOU DO?

The strategies you have just identified for these situations will give you important information about how you use your memory. Did you think of more than one strategy for each exercise or did you use the same one for all four? If you were unable to describe how you remember in one or two of them, it may indicate that you are not using many different memory techniques in your daily life or that you are not aware of the ones you do use.

The memory techniques that follow have worked for other people and may work for you as well. Here, I will simply introduce you to the range of strategies, from easy to challenging, that are useful for these four tasks. The next chapter describes the best methods in detail. Compare the recommended techniques with the methods you used for the exercises to discover your weaknesses—failure to apply appropriate strategies—as well as your strengths—effective applications of good memory techniques.

TO REMEMBER NEW INFORMATION

You could use any of the following methods to memorize what happens to your memory as you get older. To be certain that you remember, you can use more than one or even all of them:

1. Read the material aloud.
2. Read it again and again.
3. Describe the memory changes in your own words.
4. Make two lists, one of memory abilities that decline and one of memory abilities that do not decline with age.
5. Alphabetize the lists.
6. Create an interesting or bizarre sentence in which each word in the sentence begins with the same letter as a word on the list:

Your list of maintained abilities might include forgetting rates, immediate memory, world knowledge, interference, and search.

Your sentence mnemonic could be: FORGET IT, KNOWING IS STABLE. This sentence incorporates two of the maintained abilities, forgetting rates, and world knowledge, and uses the term "stable" to help you recall that these abilities remain stable as you age.

7. Think about these memory abilities in relation to your own life. What changes have you experienced? What could you do to prevent memory problems?

8. Imagine conversations with your friends. Think about how you would reassure them by describing the differences between normal changes and changes associated with poor health.

9. Think about portrayals of aging that you have seen on television, and see if what you have learned fits the media portrayal.

TO REMEMBER TO DO SOMETHING

To remember errands or tasks, some of these same methods or several new ones could be applied.

1. Write yourself a list and post it where you will see it.

2. Use the first letters of the list words to make a sentence. (Organize the list in the order in which you plan to do the tasks.)

3. Give yourself regular verbal reminders of your errands or repeatedly visualize yourself doing these three things.

4. Put cues in visible places: a pill bottle (to remind you to go to the hospital), your suit or a tie that you usually wear with it (the cleaners), and a catalog from which you may order your present.

5. Visualize all the above cues at the same time: the suit, with a huge pill bottle in the pocket, literally jumping out of the catalog. Think of this strange picture often and you definitely will not forget your three chores.

6. Use the "peg system" of memory or the "method of loci." (Both will be described in Chapter 7.)

TO REMEMBER HABITUAL ROUTINES

Most people are not aware of remembering their keys or purse or wallet. They remember automatically. Others have made it routine to ask themselves, "Do I have my keys?" before locking the door. I find that sometimes I am aware of asking myself this question, whereas on other days I unconsciously check for my keys.

Although you may remember your keys habitually now, at some time in your life it was not a habit. In my case, I had to learn to carry my keys when I moved into a college dormitory. I was lucky someone was there to rescue me when I needed it because I was forever locking myself out. The point is, whether or not you are aware of it, habits involve memory and are an important part of your memory strategy repertoire.

These are strategies you can use to establish the habit of taking this book with you when you leave the house for the next five days (you can use similar strategies for whatever habit you want to learn or reinforce):

1. Associate the book with what you plan to do by repeating to yourself: I'LL NEVER GET MY WORK DONE WITHOUT *MEMORY FITNESS*. WHATEVER I DO TODAY, I NEED *MEMORY FITNESS*.

2. Place the book in a prominent place by the door. If you already pick up your purse or keys on the way out, put the book close to them.

3. Create a mental image that will make you visualize the book as soon as you see the door. You could imagine a large book attached to the center of the door.

4. Put the book under an alarm clock set for the time you plan to leave the house that day.

5. Put a large note, BOOK, on the door.

TO REMEMBER PAST EVENTS

There are many useful techniques for recalling the past:

1. Think back to your last Thanksgiving dinner and visualize the faces around the table.

2. Try to recall the dinner conversation.

3. If you normally take pictures, look through your photo album. Try to recall the events surrounding each of the photographs. If you're lucky, you may have pictures taken at each place your aunt visited.

4. If you keep old letters, you may find that your aunt's thank-you note lists some of the places you saw together.

5. Ask friends and family members. Even if they do not remember the details of her visit, their recollections may jog your memory.

Subjective Methods of Evaluation

You can gain greater awareness of how you use your memory by keeping a diary or checklist in which you record daily memory activities, the strategies you use, and notations about the success or failure of each strategy. These subjective evaluations may be a lot of work, but they will make you more aware of the kinds of memory activities that are difficult or easy for you and will help you see how your memory functions on a day-to-day basis.

It is too easy to focus on failures, especially if you are worrying about getting old. A diary or checklist can help you become more aware of the huge number of successes you have.

KEEP A MEMORY DIARY

A memory diary is a daily log of any activities that require you to remember information. Here is a sample of one day's entries. It comes from a diary I obtained in a recent study.

> While drinking my morning coffee, I thought about what I needed to do today. I need to go to the grocery store and pharmacy, so I looked through the pantry and made a list of what I needed, and wrote my prescription number at the top of the list so I could refill it.

> Needed to make copies of a memo to distribute. Was unable to go to copy machine at the time so I got my copy card out of my desk drawer (where I always keep it) and put it on the top of my file so I would see it, and make the copies later.

> Was talking to Rita on the telephone at lunch. I invited her to stop by later today. When I got off the telephone, Henry came by and reminded me about this afternoon's staff meeting. I had forgotten.

> I was ready to go to the store. I looked over the list and remembered that I had coupons for some of the things I needed. I

had to hunt for them since I don't keep the coupons in any one place. I found them.

Was watching HBO, "Bad News Bears," and started thinking about my family and my visit in March. Thought about our last telephone conversation and recalled that I never sent them the pictures we took. I got out the negatives and put them on my nightstand so I could take them in tomorrow.

I always keep my vitamins next to my toothpaste and I remembered tonight, as usual, to take them before I brushed my teeth.

To be most helpful, your diary should contain at least three entries each day for a week or else a running record for one whole day. Make complete entries that describe your memory tasks and how you did them. If you choose to keep a diary for only one day, make sure that it is a typical day. You should consciously try to write about the full range of memory activities that you do regularly.

MAKE A BEHAVIOR CHECKLIST

An alternative to keeping a diary is to make yourself a behavior checklist. List the most common types of memory tasks you do and note your success or failure for each.

Your list need not be exhaustive; just pick the first fifteen to twenty-five memory activities that come to mind. They will probably be your most important ones. Your list might include the following:

> recognize face
> remember pill
> use arithmetic correctly
> locate item used occasionally
> learn to use new equipment
> remember recipe
> keep appointment
> send card
> communicate message
> remember specific meal

recall name
know way to store (office, home)
locate item used daily
dial phone number
complete errand
recall conversation
remember news story
reminisce
report autobiographical information
memorize song or reading

List each memory activity on the left side of a sheet of lined paper, writing on every other line. Across the top of the page, write the days of the week, evenly spaced. Draw vertical lines between the days, and horizontal lines between the memory items to make a box for each item each day. To use the checklist, write an "S" for each memory success and an "M" for each mistake in the appropriate box.

At the end of the day, think back over your memory activities. On one day you might record an S by "report autobiographical information" because you easily recalled your employment history on a job application form; an S by "recall name" because you didn't have trouble remembering any names; an M beside "memorize song or reading" because you had considerable difficulty memorizing the new personnel policies, and beside "reminisce" because you were unable to remember who spoke at your high school graduation ceremony.

An alternate way of keeping a checklist is to make an extensive record for one hour each day, selecting a different time from one day to the next.

Monday morning, you drive to work and say hello to your secretary by name—give yourself an S for knowing the way to work and two S's for recognizing your secretary's face and recalling her name. You cannot recall something important you need to do that day, so give yourself an M for not completing an errand. You couldn't recall the news story in the morning newspaper that you wanted to mention to one of your colleagues, so give yourself an M for not remembering a news story. If you think about what you ate for breakfast in order to cue yourself to the story (whether it works or not), you get an S for remembering the meal.

Your checklist will be more valuable if you make strategy notations by each entry:

You remember your secretary's face and name because you see her so often (repetition). You cannot recall the errand because you wrote yourself a note about it and you can't find the note (writing). You used organization to help you remember the newspaper story, but it didn't work. You used visualization to recall breakfast.

WHAT DID YOU LEARN ABOUT YOUR MEMORY?

This subjective look at your memory should give you some idea about its breadth and flexibility. The diary or checklist should help you gain some perspective on your own abilities and see the relationship between the application of strategies and your daily memory skill.

Did mental pictures come to mind easily and aid your memory? Use mental pictures more often.

Did you forget things when you used mental pictures? Practice to improve their accuracy and distinctiveness because distinct mental pictures are easier to remember than vague ones.

Were your successes based on verbal rather than visual techniques? Work toward improving verbal elaboration and letter associations (see Chapter 7).

Did you forget your doctor's appointment because you thought you'd remember without trying, and so you applied no effort? Next time make the effort.

Did you forget errands that you repeated in your mind? Next time try using visible cues to remind you.

Did you mainly remember information you wrote down? Use notes more often as a backup.

Did you write notes to yourself and then lose them? You need a memory place for your notes (see Chapter 7).

Did you forget an important meeting because you didn't put it on your calendar, thinking instead that rehearsing it in your head would be enough? You need to establish a calendar habit (see Chapter 11).

Test Your Memory Power

Your final assignment for self-evaluation is to test yourself. The eight tests given here examine your ability to memorize and recall information in a structured setting. They will help you learn more about your strengths and weaknesses because they test the limits of your ability. The tests are all in written form, so you will still have to rely on your diary or checklist to evaluate your ability to remember pictures, sounds, or other nonverbal information.

GENERAL INSTRUCTIONS

Find a quiet room (or a quiet time) in your home so you can concentrate. If necessary, take two or three tests each day on different days. Have a pad of paper and a pencil available to record your answers. To make sure that you understand what you are supposed to do, read through the entire description for each test at least once before starting it.

After you finish a test ask yourself what internal memory strategy you used to recall the information, and make a note of it. This information will aid in your evaluation. Unless I specifically instruct you to do so, do not check your answers until you have finished all the tests. If you want a useful self-assessment, don't peek!

TEST 1

See if you can remember the large items of furniture in one room in your house, preferably the living room or family room. Write down each item as you remember it.

Do not check your accuracy until you have finished all the tests. Do not continue reading until you have done this test.

TEST 2

This test assesses your ability to carry out instructions. I will ask you to get 5 objects and take each one to another location in your house. Read through the instructions only once, very carefully, but do not study them for any length of time. As soon as you have finished reading, go get the objects and place them in the specified locations; do not check back with the book.

Here are your instructions. Read the entire list before you begin.

Go get your COMB and get your TOOTHBRUSH.

Place your COMB on top of the STOVE and place your TOOTHBRUSH inside the REFRIGERATOR.

Get your TELEPHONE BOOK and put it on your BED.

Get some TAPE (any kind that is close by) and a PAPER OR PLASTIC BAG.

Put the TAPE on the nearest TABLE.

Put the BAG on the kitchen COUNTER.

Get a GLASS from the KITCHEN and place it by the BATH-ROOM SINK.

Do not continue until you have carried out the instructions.

After you have finished, check yourself. See if each object is in its designated location. Make a note of your errors, then complete any tasks that you forgot. Leave the objects in their new locations because later you will be asked to recall where they are.

TEST 3

Here is a list of words to remember. Read the list only once, slowly and aloud, but do not study it for any length of time. After you have read the words, close the book, and write down the words you can recall; they do not have to be in order.

Read the list and try to recall it now.

WITCH	LAMP
CHERRY	ROCK
JADE	BONNET
FLOOR	DRILL
HONEY	CLAW
NOOSE	TIRE
FIDDLE	PAIL
SHEEP	DAISY
BOAT	KNIFE
GRIN	MINER

Later, you will check the accuracy of your recall. *Go on to the next test.*

TEST 4

This test involves prospective memory—remembering to do something specific that has been planned for a later time. I want you to do a task after you finish the next two memory tests. The next two tests are a phone number recall test (Test 5) and an object location recall test (Test 6).

When you have completed those two tests, and not before, write down four things:

YOUR COMPLETE ADDRESS
YOUR HOME PHONE NUMBER
YOUR BIRTH DATE
THE FULL NAME OF YOUR CLOSEST RELATIVE

Do not write these now and do not look back here to remind yourself. *Go on to the next test.*

TEST 5

For this test you have to remember phone numbers. Look in the yellow pages of your telephone directory for the phone numbers of the *first three* florists listed. Memorize the numbers; you may take up to three minutes to study them. Then close the phone book, and call each one to inquire about the price of a single red rose in a vase (picked up, not delivered). Don't engage the first florist in conversation or you may forget the other phone numbers. Do not write down the phone numbers—use internal memory. If you misdial, you will soon find out! Keep your pad and pencil handy to note any misdialed numbers, so you can see later how close you were to the actual phone numbers.

Get your phone book now, and learn the numbers for the first three florists. Do not continue until you have finished this test.

TEST 6

This test requires you to recall the locations of objects in your home. If you have more than one of any object, identify the nearest one. Skip any item that you do not have. Some of these objects were moved in Test 2, so they will not be in their usual places. You may write down the object locations one at a time and refer to the list below as you write your answers.

Write from memory the exact location (including the specific drawer or shelf section) of the following:

ADDRESS BOOK (OR CALENDAR)
YELLOW PAGES OF THE TELEPHONE BOOK
SCISSORS
SCOTCH TAPE (OR OTHER TAPE)
COMB
CAN OPENER
PAPER OR PLASTIC CUPS
STATIONERY
ADDING MACHINE OR CALCULATOR
PENCIL SHARPENER
DICTIONARY
SWIMMING CAP OR GOGGLES

TEST 7

This test involves remembering an ordinary grocery list. I want you to read the list, and then go into the kitchen and take these things off your shelves or out of your refrigerator. You need to find only one of each item, and you do not need to recall the list in order. Read through the grocery list carefully two times, close the book, and then go to your kitchen to find the items. If a particular item is not in your kitchen at all, write it down when you recall it.

Read the following list twice:

MILK	PLASTIC BAGS
SUGAR	LETTUCE
CANNED SOUP	EGGS
APPLES	COFFEE
GROUND BEEF	ORANGES
CHEESE	BACON
CORN	NAPKINS
BREAD	JUICE

Go to your kitchen now and find these items.

When you have finished, bring this book into the kitchen and check to see how many items you recalled. After writing down your score, you can put away your groceries.

TEST 4A

Did you remember to write out some information about yourself before beginning the grocery list test? If not, do it now.

Do not go back to read the Test 4 instructions. If you have not already done so, write the information now.

TEST 8

This test examines your ability to recall a set of doctor's instructions. You may wish to pretend that your doctor is giving them to you. The best way to take this test is to ask someone to read the passage to you or record it on a tape recorder. After you listen to the instructions, write them on your pad. If you are alone, read them aloud and then write them on your pad.

Here are the doctor's instructions:

"This should have you feeling better in four or five days. I'm writing you a prescription for erythromycin. You can take it to the pharmacy on the corner if you want. The bottle will tell you how often to take them. Make sure that you take them ALL.

"Buy some Sinutab for your congestion. Take two Sinutabs every six hours for a week, or as long as the congestion lasts.

"Drink lots of fluids. If your fever is not gone within 48 hours, call me again."

Do the test before you continue.

Evaluating Your Performance

The tests you just took are not simple tests of memory. They were constructed to challenge your ability. Your performance, of course, depends upon the memory strategies you applied and your ability to concentrate.

Spend a few minutes now checking over your answers for each test and thinking about the strategies you used. I will give you some general guidelines for determining how well you have done, and I will describe some memory techniques you could have used.

TEST 1

This test shows you how well you can remember information that has had many reviews. Typically, such information is easy to remember. Unless you have moved recently, you have looked at your furniture and appliances many times. You should have remembered 4 out of 5 items, but if you had over 20 to recall, your percentage may be smaller.

Visualization is probably the best strategy for this test. If you were able to see the room in your mind, you may have recalled everything. Many people find that they can actually imagine walking through the room, noting the pieces of furniture they see as they "walk" by them.

TEST 2

These instructions contained 12 tasks if you count getting the object, and placing the object, as two separate tasks. You should have completed at least 8 of them without looking back at the book. You may have had problems if you did not know where some things were located. If you couldn't find the telephone book, for example, you may have forgotten the rest of the instructions while you were hunting for it!

There are many possible strategies that could help you to remember the instructions:

Combined rehearsal. Repeat the instructions in your mind, adding new items as you read along. At the same time, abbreviate each specific task to its shortest form: GET COMB AND TOOTHBRUSH, TAKE TO STOVE AND REFRIGERATOR, then later, COMB, TOOTHBRUSH TO STOVE, FRIDGE, PHONE BOOK TO BED, and later, COMB, TOOTH, STOVE, FRIDGE, BOOK-BED, TAPE-TABLE, and so on. You can only read and do combined rehearsal in your mind at the same time if you read the series very slowly.

Visualization. Visualize each of the objects in its new location. This strategy should be possible even with a quick reading of the instructions.

First letter associations. You want to remember that the comb goes to the stove, so you could use the word CAST. Remember that the toothbrush goes to the refrigerator with the word TAR, and that the book goes to the bed with the word BOB.

Verbal elaboration. Now combine these words into a meaningful sentence: CAST TAR AT BOB. Elaboration takes time unless you have practiced it. But with extensive practice, the technique will become automatic, and you will be able to use it efficiently and rapidly.

TEST 3

You can feel very accomplished if you remembered 15 of these 20 words. If you read through the list quickly, you probably remembered only 8 to 10 because the words are not related to each other in any way and they are not all easy to picture mentally.

Combined rehearsal and *verbal elaboration* are useful for remembering word lists.

Interactive imagery. This is probably the best strategy. You first visualize the witch, lamp, cherry, rock, jade, and bonnet. Then combine these pictures into one meaningful scene. For example, you could imagine a WITCH wearing a large BONNET sitting by a LAMP. The WITCH throws the JADE stone at a CHERRY that is on a ROCK. This interactive image will help you to remember 6 of the words on the list. The fewer images you create, the better.

TEST 4

Prospective memory has rarely been studied systematically. In my studies, I have found that about 70 percent of the people remember prospective tasks on time. You should have recalled at least 3 of the 4 items you were asked to write down since they were all personal data that you are used to writing on applications or medical forms.

External aids, such as lists or object cues are the most effective way to recall everyday prospective memory tasks. However, this was a test of internal memory.

Association is an internal strategy that would help you. If you regard 7 as a lucky number, you could say to yourself: WHEN I SEE TEST 7, I WRITE DOWN MY PERSONAL INFORMATION BECAUSE 7 IS MY PERSONAL LUCKY NUMBER. You could also imagine a very elaborately drawn 7 with curlicues to associate writing or drawing with a 7.

TEST 5

You had a head start if you live in a city with very few phone exchanges. The phone number test included memory for well-learned information (the exchanges) as well as new information (the particular combination of digits used in the numbers). You should have correctly dialed at least one entire number and part of the other two. If the three exchanges were the same, your score ought to be 100 percent.

Repetition. Short-term memory for phone numbers can be accomplished most easily by simply repeating them a few times in your mind until you dial them. The effectiveness of this method depends on the simplicity and similarity of the numbers.

You could enhance your ability to remember any three phone numbers by using either of these two techniques:

Chunking. This is a type of organization. A 7-digit number has seven separate units to remember, but it has only two parts to organize, the exchange and the last four digits. Chunking means grouping the digits into units that are easy to remember.

The exchange can be remembered as one unit if you are familiar with it. The last four digits can be recalled as two 2-digit numbers rather than four 1-digit numbers. Don't say the number to yourself as 3-8-1-6-5-2-9, but 381-65-29. If all of the numbers in your city typically begin with 38, you need only rehearse 1-65-29. The fewer separate new numbers you need to recall, the better.

Mathematical relationships between numbers. The number 381-6529 has a 3 followed by two digits, then a 6 followed by two more digits, then a 9. All three of these—3, 6, and 9—are divisible by 3. You could also note that the number next to the 3 is one less than 9, and the number next to the 9 is one less than 3.

If you practice thinking about numbers in this way, you will speed up your ability to recognize such relationships. Typically, this kind of examination of phone numbers is necessary only when you wish to remember a new number for a long time, or you need to remember several numbers at once.

TEST 6

If you have not already done so, go look for the 12 objects in the locations you specified. Do not give yourself credit for a correct answer unless the object is exactly where you expected to find it (in the third drawer, not the second). Just as in Test 1, this test relied mainly on well-learned information, except for the objects that were moved during Test 2. Most people can pinpoint locations for at least 10 of these commonly used household items. Several methods will increase your ability to recall object locations.

Organize your environment. If you follow "a place for everything and everything in its place," this test was probably easy for you. In fact, people who have very well-organized homes may get every one correct.

If you had trouble remembering the locations of objects that were not moved earlier, you may be living under an increased memory load, which means that you probably have to hunt for things too often. You may wish to establish permanent locations for household items—memory places—so that you can find them easily when you need them.

Mental imagery. You may have had difficulty remembering the current location of the objects you moved during Test 2. It may help to associate items with their locations through imagery. If you put your glasses on the TV set, you could imagine the TV screen as the frame in a huge pair of glasses.

Verbal elaboration. You could also associate the object with its location with verbal elaboration: I NEED MY GLASSES TO SEE THE TV. IF I HIT IT, THE TV SCREEN WOULD SHATTER JUST LIKE MY GLASSES.

TEST 7

You should have recalled 10 to 12 of these 16 grocery items. They are fairly easy to remember because they are common purchases that can easily be pictured in your mind. You could even imagine these products in their normal grocery-shelf locations.

Interactive imagery, verbal elaboration, and *combined rehearsal* will all aid recall.

Organization. You can recall lists like this by organizing items into common categories (fruits together, dairy products together) or categories based on spatial relationships (fresh fruits and vegetables are both in the produce section). You could organize according to your usual route through the grocery store.

TEST 8

The doctor's instructions involved new information and some typical advice. You should have remembered about 10 of these 20 "facts." Check yourself against this list:

Should have you feeling better
In 4 or 5 days
Writing a prescription
For erythromycin
Take it to the pharmacy

On the corner
Bottle will tell you (something)
How often to take them
Take them all
Buy (something)
(Buy) Sinutab
For congestion
Take 2
Every 6 hours
For a week
As long as congestion lasts
Drink fluids
If fever not gone
Within 48 hours
Call me again

It is necessary to isolate these facts for scoring because you might recall that the doctor asked you to call him but not the reason why. Give yourself one point for each separate "fact" you wrote down.

Organization. To remember this set of instructions, it would be helpful to organize them in some way. You could link together meaningful elements in your mind by noting that the doctor begins with when you will feel better, goes through prescription and non-prescription medicines, then tells you what to do if you don't feel better.

If you can remember that sequence, you could also recall the associated number sequence: 4 TO 5 DAYS (to feel better), ALL (prescription medicine), 2 EVERY 6 HOURS (non-prescription medicine), and 48 HOURS (to call if still feverish).

Interactive imagery. You could link together elements with mental images. For example, to remember that you'll feel better in four or five days by taking erythromycin, you could picture a happy 4 and 5 dancing (because they feel good!) to a rhythm (erythromycin). This absurd picture will be memorable, and you may be able to add other elements from the directions.

You will not need to make any special effort to recall some parts of the directions because you probably know them already (you may already know that Sinutab is for congestion, or that you should take all of the erythromycin because it is an antibiotic).

WHAT TO DO NOW

Now that you have had a memory workout that included four memory tasks, a diary or checklist, and a memory test, you should be aware of how you use your memory. Even if you did not complete all the exercises, reading them may have motivated you to consider new methods to accomplish more memory tasks. Look over the results to evaluate your strengths and weaknesses, and keep them in mind as you learn more about improving your memory power.

What If You Didn't Remember As Much As You Expected?

You may have noticed strategies that you do not apply very well. If you found that you recalled well-learned information but not new information, practice strategies for learning. If you had difficulty recalling well-learned information, practice retrieval strategies.

Perhaps you have allowed yourself to live without any memory demands for too long. You should plan to increase mental stimulation and challenge your memory on a regular basis. Perhaps you were not feeling well. Evaluate yourself again when you are feeling better.

If you lacked self-confidence and gave up on some tasks, you should try to achieve some minor memory successes to bolster your self-concept: learn three names, memorize the peg system, recall the headlines in today's newspaper. If your memory is overloaded, try to set priorities.

If none of these explanations seems likely, and you are concerned about your performance, you may want to get a more complete evaluation of your memory ability from a psychologist.

What If You Did Better Than You Expected?

Your self-evaluation should indicate the kinds of memory tasks or situations that are easy for you. You may have discovered a number of strategies in your repertoire that you were not aware of using.

Perhaps your expectations were low because an unconscious acceptance of stereotypes about aging has led you to focus too much on failures and too little on successes. Try to change your attitude.

Any strategies that consistently led to high recall on these exercises should be used as backup when you practice other methods or when you cannot afford to forget. If none stands out, practice all the strategies described in this book until you can identify those that help you remember better.

No matter how well you did, don't relax your efforts to maintain the highest possible memory power. There's always room for improvement, for everyone.

7

Memory Strategies

Once you have gained a sense of your memory strengths and weaknesses, you should begin learning some strategies to improve your ability. Even if you don't feel as if you have any specific memory problems, these strategies will increase your overall memory power, no matter what your age.

Some of the strategies described in this chapter can improve retention and recall. Most of the strategies, however, are designed to improve learning ability, because most of what has been written about memory improvement has focused on learning. Learning is the first phase of remembering, and your ability to retain and recall depends, in part, on the effectiveness of initial learning. If information is not learned well in the first place, retention and recall are not likely to be successful.

Keep in mind as you read about these techniques that many of them were developed by memory experts to help them recall masses of information. That is probably not your goal. But the same techniques are equally applicable for recalling smaller amounts of information in your everyday world, and they can substantially increase your memory power once you are able to use them with ease.

Samuel Johnson once said, "The art of memory is the art of attention." If you don't pay attention to something in the first place, you will not be able to remember it, no matter what strategies you try to apply later. The strategies in this chapter focus on techniques for remembering once your attention has already been captured.

INTERNAL STRATEGIES

Internal strategies for learning include the following:
> Rote repetition
> Verbal elaboration
> Organization
> Mental imagery
> Association

You may have used some of these when you were a student, or you may use them now, without thinking of them as memory strategies. Other strategies will be new to you and will be somewhat more difficult to learn and apply, but they work so well that it's worth taking time to master them.

Rote Repetition

Many people depend on repetition as their primary learning tool. You are using rote repetition when you see or hear something and copy it right back. Someone says to you, "Please give this message to Carl when you see him—call Mr. Bronson in accounting," and you repeat to yourself: I HAVE TO GIVE THIS MESSAGE TO CARL WHEN I SEE HIM—CALL MR. BRONSON IN ACCOUNTING. You use rote repetition when you mentally repeat the phone number given to you by the operator, or read a list of names aloud several times to memorize it.

Short-term learning. Rote repetition is effective for short-term learning. When someone gives you a sales figure to use in a report and all you have to do is go to your office and write it down, *without ever using it again,* your best bet is simply to repeat that number a few times to yourself as you walk down the hall. You can remember the title and university degrees of someone you have to introduce at a banquet by repeating them over and over until you make the introduction.

Long-term learning. For long-term learning, on the other hand, repetition is a weak technique. You are more likely to retain information for a long time after you reorganize, code, or elaborate it. All of the other internal strategies described in this chapter help you to perform these mental transformations that make information more meaningful.

Verbal Elaboration

You create elaborations by adding verbal information to items as you memorize them. Words or names that you want to remember become parts of a memorable sentence that builds on and associates those words. Sentences or ideas may be combined into a story or poem. Numbers may be coded as consonants and—with vowels added—transformed into words.

Verbal elaboration can be used to remember almost anything, but it is most successful as a memory technique when it gives meaning to something that was not previously meaningful or when it adds information that is specifically related to what you want to remember.

ADD MEANING TO NONMEANINGFUL MATERIAL

You often have to memorize information that has no intrinsic meaning. It is sometimes hard, for example, to attach meanings to peoples' names. Numbers and dates lack meaning unless you are skilled at noting mathematical relationships.

Usually, when you study or begin to work in a new field, you are expected to learn a vocabulary composed of words you have never seen before. In a beginning course in psychology, for example, you have to learn the definitions of terms such as "id" or "libido." If you start to work in a hospital, you may be required to memorize anatomical terms or names of drugs. When you begin taking music lessons, you have to learn the names of the notes on the musical staff and the meaning of "crescendo" and other terms.

To be successful with these kinds of memory tasks:

Look for meaningful words embedded in whatever information you are trying to learn.

Add information that incorporates the word(s) into a phrase or sentence that is easy to store in your head.

Names such as Scheider and Watkins may not have meaning for you. But you can remember the name Scheider by thinking of SHY DEER and the name Watkins by WATT (bulb) CANS.

You can elaborate on the term "id" (Freud's term for people's unconscious drives and desires) by thinking to yourself: THE ID IS HID.

You might remember "libido" (Freud's term for sexual instincts) by making up a sentence such as: HE HAD A LID ON HIS LIBIDO.

Suppose that you had to remember the medical term "blepharo," a prefix referring to the eyelids. You could relate the definition of the word to its sound with a sentence such as: I'D BLINK IF I SAW THE PHAROAH.

Generations of music students have used EVERY GOOD BOY DOES FINE to learn the notes on the staff.

Crescendo means "to get louder," so you can remember its meaning by saying: I'M CLIMBING TO THE TOP OF THE CRESCENT.

Numbers and dates can be elaborated on as well. A familiar elaboration for numbers is the rhyme "Thirty days hath September."

To remember a 2 o'clock dentist appointment, you can say: I'M BLUE AT TWO.

To recall your wedding date, August 17, 1976, you could quip: IN 1776 THE BRITISH AND WE GOT FIXED.

MAKE MEANINGFUL MATERIAL MORE MEMORABLE

You often have to remember information that is already meaningful, such as the points to make in a speech. You can use verbal elaboration to link any items you want to recall.

Imagine that you have been asked to make a speech honoring a friend of yours for his years of service to the Boys' Club. These are the points you want to remember:

He has been an effective fundraiser and a good organizer.

He has devoted thousands of volunteer hours to unpopular jobs.

He has been an inspiration to young people.

He has been good at resolving conflicts.

You could easily write out the main points on an index card, but you'd prefer to give the speech without notes. You can remember this list by using verbal elaboration.

Say to yourself: HE SOLVED CONFLICTS BY VOLUNTEERING TO ORGANIZE FUNDS FOR YOUNG PEOPLE. This sentence adds to the information you need to recall in a way that links the points in your mind.

Verbal elaboration can also be used to make isolated pieces of information more memorable. For example, a joke punch line may be difficult to remember because it's not related directly to the sentence preceding it (that's what makes the joke funny). For the line, "The fat woman bought some scissors," you don't need to make the sentence meaningful, but you do need help in recalling exactly what the woman bought. The most successful elaborations are specific. You could say to yourself: THE FAT WOMAN BOUGHT SOME

SCISSORS . . . SO SHE COULD CUT CALORIES. An elaboration such as, "The fat woman bought some scissors . . . to do her sewing," will not improve recall because it does not link her weight with her purchase.

You might think that verbal elaborations make learning harder because they add more information, but this is not the case; by enhancing meaning and putting all that you need to learn into one cohesive unit, the added information makes remembering considerably easier.

Organization

You can use organization to combine several pieces of information into a group or multiple groupings. Words or pictures can be categorized by similarity of type (animals, furniture, vehicles) or physical characteristics such as shape or color. You can also organize information according to time or location (morning, San Francisco, bedroom), family or social connections (upper class, working class), sounds (rock music, opera), movements (gross motor, fine motor tasks), or any other logical relationship. Any time you can make yourself aware of relationships or impose a logical order on information, recall is easier.

ORGANIZATION BY TYPE

Whenever you have a number of related items or activities to remember, such as errands or purchases, try to organize them into categories.

Suppose that you have several things to do immediately before leaving on your vacation: take the dog to the kennel, take the cat to the neighbors, turn off the lamp, turn off the stove, pack the car with food and maps, pack the boat with life vests and suntan oil, and make sure you have your suitcase, wallet, and backpack.

You can reduce the list to DOG, CAT, LAMP, STOVE, CAR, BOAT, SUITCASE, WALLET, BACKPACK. Then divide the list into categories and say to yourself:

ANIMALS—2
HOUSE—2
PACKING—2 BY 2
POSSESSIONS—3

You can remember that you have four categories of things to do before you leave, with two tasks in each category, except the possessions category, and two things to pack in each of your two packing places.

ORGANIZATION BY LEVEL OF IMPORTANCE

Hierarchical organization is a useful way to remember written materials, since they can usually be divided into components that are higher level (topic sentence, main point) or lower level (specific example, inference).

The instruction manual for operating a piece of equipment may cover "main functions," "basic operating instructions," "trouble shooting," and "parts." If the manual is not organized in this fashion, it is even more important that you identify those topics. You could even outline each of these topics as a memory aid. Then, you could memorize the five steps needed to operate the equipment. You may also find it useful to identify and memorize troubleshooting information for the most common problems that can occur, so you won't have to consult the manual for every little problem. If you do not need to remember the names of specific parts, you can omit them from your outline.

PQRST METHOD

This is a variant on hierarchical organization. The letters PQRST stand for Preview, Question, Read, State, Test. This is how it works:

Preview: Look over the reading briefly to identify the main points.

Question: Develop questions that specify what it is you want to learn or retain from the reading.

Read: Read the material carefully.

State: State or repeat the central ideas.

Test: Try to answer your questions.

This method encourages you to notice the organization of the text and read in a focused way. The questions provide organization because you will examine everything you read in relation to the answers you are seeking.

ORGANIZATION BY PROXIMITY

When you need to recall things in order, you can organize by proximity. For instance, you can remember the phone number 396-1710 as THREE NINETY-SIX . . . SEVENTEEN . . . TEN by grouping the digits into three, rather than seven numbers.

Similarly, you can use spatial proximity—the layout of the store—to organize a shopping list. Then, if you drop by the supermarket on the way home from work without your list, you can "walk" through the list in your mind as you take your usual route through the aisles. You will recognize most of what you need.

Mental Imagery

A picture in your mind is called a mental image. People commonly use imagery to remember, even though they may not be aware of it. If I asked you to describe the outside of your house, you would probably start by forming a mental picture of the house. To describe your best friend, you would probably try to picture his/her face, and to remember where you parked your car this morning, you might try to imagine yourself driving into the parking lot.

Mental pictures can be used to remember words, faces, pictures, diagrams, buildings, and actions, as well as to connect items in a list or to connect people's names with their appearance.

BEST TYPES OF IMAGES

The more clear and detailed your mental pictures, the more accurate your memory will be. Images with action in them will be retained better than static images. Distinctive images are easier to recall, so an unusual or strange picture will help you remember; however, your images need not be absurd as long as they are vivid.

INTERACTIVE IMAGERY

This technique requires you to make a mental picture that combines related items.

Kenneth wanted to impress a new client by remembering his favorite hobbies and interests. He knew that it would be awkward to take notes at their meeting, so he had to use an internal memory strategy. At first he thought he could remember a few facts by saying over and over to himself: JOE SMITH LOVES FOOTBALL AND SAILING. But he discovered that this was an ineffective strategy for long-term memory, especially since he had many clients. Instead, he pictured Joe climbing up the goalposts carrying a sail.

Kenneth also could have imagined his client sailing down the football field in a sailboat. He could remember the client's wife's occupation by picturing her in a job-related activity, such as pounding a gavel in a courtroom or breaking a test tube in a laboratory.

Remembering a list. Combining mental pictures is a good way to remember a list. If you need tomatoes, paper towels, apples, butter, and stationery and you don't want to bother making a list, you could say these five things over and over in your head, but that would be a waste of mental effort. Instead, construct a distinctive interactive image; to be most effective, the image should incorporate items into action sequences. Let the image run through your mind like a video.

A plump tomato with arms is wiping off a counter with paper towels. In comes Johnny Appleseed sowing seeds right and left. The tomato is annoyed at the mess and throws a butter container at Johnny, who runs out and writes a letter of complaint to the city officials that his program is not being supported by the community.

This strange story connects all five items on the list. A simpler but perhaps less memorable tale could be the following:

> The tomato and apple are using paper towels and stationery to clean up butter spilled on the floor.

It doesn't matter what kind of story you make up, just as long as it places all of the items on your list into one distinctive interactive image. A mental picture of yourself talking to a client about his interests or picking up five items at the store would be too ordinary to be memorable.

IMAGERY FOR ACTIONS

Imagery can be very effective for remembering action sequences or specific movements. As the installer shows you how to operate your new VCR, try to visualize the process in your mind. After you practice the operational sequence, close your eyes and imagine yourself doing it. You should be able to visualize your own movements as if you were watching yourself.

Athletes sometimes use this technique to evaluate their performance. They create a mental image of the stroke or foot placement they want to achieve and compare that image to what they are actually doing with their bodies.

Association

Association—connecting new information to something you already know—is a natural part of the way memory works. It is through association that old memories suddenly pop into your mind. Those memories are somehow related to the experience you are having at the moment. Many psychologists believe that our memories are stored in association networks.

My favorite personal example is an association based on a distinct smell and "feel" in the air.

I once lived in Glasgow, Scotland, where there is a constant mist in the air. Glasgow is an old industrial city, with a diesel fuel smell from trucks and buses concentrated in the city center. One damp, misty day when I was back home in America, a truck drove by and backfired. The diesel smell, combined with the dampness, "transported" me to George Square in Glasgow. I was suddenly reminded of the buildings, the people, and the hustle and bustle of the city. Through association, many other memories of Glasgow came flooding back.

You probably have had similar "sense" associations, as when a certain melody, smell or taste calls to mind an entire experience. *People in context.* You often associate people with the locations where you see them. That is why you have a hard time recognizing the gasoline station attendant in the drug store. You know that the face is familiar, but without the associated context, you don't have complete recognition.

You associate people with their jobs and think of Anne as a lawyer and Carl as a professor. When you see the two of them leading a Cub Scout troop, they seem somehow out of place because of the strength of your context association. By using associations as a memory aid, you can take advantage of this natural way in which memories are stored and enhance your ability to remember.

TIME ASSOCIATIONS

Time association is a method for recalling when an event took place by associating it with the dates of salient personal events.

Suppose that you are trying to remember what year your parents moved to Florida. You can use your own life event dates as guideposts. Make a list of as many dates and events as you can remember, in this manner, trying to associate your parents' activities to each item:

     1958—Graduated from college
     1963—John F. Kennedy was assassinated
     1965—Got married
     1969—First man on the moon
     1970—My first child was born

Letter Associations

Letter associations can be used to remember many things. One technique is to link particular letters or letter sounds to numbers, creating a code. Another technique is to use verbal elaboration to build a sentence or word from the first letters of words you want to recall.

Coding numbers. You can remember a number by first associating its digits with the appropriate letters and then using verbal elaboration to translate the letters into words or sentences. The code must be well memorized and practiced before the system can work.

$$0 = \text{S, Z}$$
$$1 = \text{T}$$
$$2 = \text{N}$$
$$3 = \text{M}$$
$$4 = \text{R}$$
$$5 = \text{L}$$
$$6 = \text{Ch, Sh}$$
$$7 = \text{hard C, G, K}$$
$$8 = \text{F, Ph, V}$$
$$9 = \text{B, D, P}$$

To remember the phone number 902-6744, translate the numbers into PSN-ChKRR and recall it as POISON CHECKER, or DZN-ShKRR and recall it as DOZEN SHAKER.

Since each sound has only one number associated with it, you should be able to translate your words back into numbers. You must be careful, though, not to put extra consonant sounds into your words. The number 902 needs to be "poison" or "pass on," and not prison or Parisian (9402).

First letter associations. To make the best use of this technique, you need to remind yourself repeatedly of the actual words for which the letters stand.

Roslyn was being interviewed for an important job and she wanted to tell the interviewer five of her best attributes. In an effort to appear polished, she decided not to use notes. She wanted to emphasize that she is a Creative thinker, is willing to Work hard, has Supervisory experience, is highly Organized, and gets along well with others (Likable). She memorized the letters C, W, S, O, and L, then used verbal elaboration to combine them into one meaningful word, SCOWL.

Roslyn has to remember that SCOWL stands for supervisory, creative, organized, works hard, and likable.

She could also use the first letter associations in a different elaboration and recall her good qualities by saying, THE OWL COMMANDED SILENCE.

My favorite example of combining first letter associations with elaboration is one I used to recall the order of the planets from the sun: MY VERY EARNEST MOTHER JUST SERVED US NINE PICKLES. It's a silly sentence but it works to establish long-term learning.

PEG SYSTEM

There are two mnemonic systems that combine association and imagery—the peg system and the method of loci. The peg system is a strategy that matches each number from 1 to 10 with an object. Before you can use it you must memorize ten objects with associated numbers.

Once you know a peg list, you can apply it anywhere, anytime you need to remember a list. My peg system goes like this:

1 is a bun
2 is a shoe
3 is a tree
4 is a door
5 is a hive
6 is sticks
7 is heaven
8 is a gate
9 is a vine
10 is a hen

To use the peg system, you simply get a mental picture of the first item on your list interacting in some way with a bun, the second item with a shoe, and so on.

You're not required to use these particular words, of course. If you have already memorized a set of objects, body parts, or pictures that correspond to the numbers from one to ten, you can use those. You may prefer to use the words from the song, "This Old Man, He Played One," or you may have mental pictures to go with "The Twelve Days of Christmas." The point is that you have to get a picture in your mind to go with at least ten numbers.

Remembering a list. Let's say that during the day you think of some errands you have to run: drop off clothes at cleaners, pick up developed photographs, give list of volunteer workers to a friend. It's not convenient to write a list, and the events are too ordinary to be easy to remember. The trick is to associate each errand to a peg, and to create a memorable image for each association:

Errand 1. Imagine a BUN (1 is a bun) as the large press at the dry cleaners.

Errand 2. Imagine a SHOE (2 is a shoe) filled with rolls of film.

Errand 3. Picture your name list written on a large TREE (3 is a tree.)

Your peg pictures need to be out of the ordinary and very clearly visualized, with details embellished. Make your pictures distinctive and meaningful. Your errands will come to mind automatically when you think of the peg objects.

The peg system is especially useful when you need to remember items in order.

Leslie wanted to remember, in order, the warm-up exercises her aerobics instructor used so she could do them at home or when she was out of town. She tried writing them down, but having to stop between each set of exercises to read the note broke the routine. The peg system was the ideal solution:

Exercise 1—reaching her arms straight up and stretching. She imagined herself reaching for a hamburger BUN hanging from the light in the center of the room.

Exercise 2—stretching down to her toes. All she had to think of was SHOE. (This one was easy.)

Exercise 3—bending at the waist forward, to the right, back, and to the left. She pictured herself attached to the branches of a huge TREE being blown by the wind in all directions.

Remembering dates. Pegs can also be used to associate tasks or events with particular days. You can even remember to pay your bills by visualizing each day in the month with a particular peg picture.

I always think of the third of the month as a huge weeping willow TREE (3 is a tree) with money hanging from its branches, because the house and car payments need to be mailed on that day. When the third comes, I think of the tree and remember to pay those bills.

I could possibly skip the peg system picture and imagine money hanging from a "3." Imagery, however, tends to work better with concrete objects rather than with abstractions such as numbers.

METHOD OF LOCI

This technique, also called the method of places, involves associating new information to familiar locations through mental imagery. Although you can apply the method to single pieces of information—for example, you might remember to make a phone call first thing in the morning by imagining the telephone resting on your toothbrush—it is generally used to recall large numbers of items.

The method of loci originated in ancient Greece. As the story goes, Simonedes left a banquet hall just before an earthquake caused the collapse of the building, killing everyone inside. The bodies were indistinguishable after the building collapsed, but Simonedes was able to identify them by recalling each person's position around the table.

To use this method, you first need to select a series of locations inside your home or along a familiar path. If you always park your car in the same parking lot when you go to work, your series of locations could be the following:
1. The car
2. The parking lot entrance
3. The maple tree on the corner
4. The guard at the building door
5. The elevator
6–12. Each desk that you pass

How would you remember to invite twelve friends from your office to a party?

One good way would be to place them in your locations in the order you're likely to see them:
Brad is sitting on top of your CAR
Ethel is doing a little dance at the PARKING LOT ENTRANCE
Phyllis is waving at you from atop the MAPLE TREE (and so on)

You would then imagine walking along this route to recall those you wanted to invite. You'd think of the first location, the CAR, and invite Brad. Next you'd think of the PARKING LOT ENTRANCE and invite Ethel. This very simple device would ensure that you didn't forget anyone.

EXTERNAL STRATEGIES

External strategies can be used for learning, retention, or recall. These are the best external strategies:

Writing notes
Organizing the environment
Using object cues

Writing Notes

It would be simple to say "write it down," and leave it at that. However, what you write and where you write (or put) it are critical factors for effective writing strategies. In addition, notes are valuable cues for recall.

Anyone who has difficulty writing, because of arthritis or some other disability, can use a tape recorder as if it were a writing pad.

For notes to be most useful, they must meet the following criteria:

Reinforce your internal strategies
Be specific
Be available when needed

REINFORCE INTERNAL STRATEGIES

The use of written notes as a memory strategy is not intended to replace your internal memory, but rather to supplement and support it. As I indicated before, written notes cannot be used without internal effort. They should be regarded not as a crutch, but as one additional element in your strategy repertoire.

Writing something down—whether or not you actually use what you have written—helps your memory:

Writing focuses your attention.
Writing provides motor cues—you move your hand to write.
Writing provides visual cues—you see what you are writing.

I take notes whenever I hear a lecture. Most of the time I throw the notes away, but I find that the act of writing forces me to identify the key points made by the speaker.

To support your internal memory, your notes should be organized in the same way as your internal categories. If you use a peg system for recalling your errands, your written list must record the items in the same order as they are linked to the pegs.

To strengthen your memory for the names of authors you want to discuss with your book club, write your list in the order of your mnemonic. Your written reminder must read Dreiser, Hemingway, Dos Passos, Fitzgerald, and Stein to reinforce the mnemonic DR. HE DOES FIT SHOES.

MAKE NOTES SPECIFIC

Notes are better memory aids when they are specific. A note like "errands tomorrow" is much less useful than DOCTOR AT 1:30, HAIR DRESSER at 3, TAKE GIFT TO POST OFFICE.

To be specific with a calendar, you need to record the place of your appointment as well as the time. If you don't automatically associate that place with a particular person or purpose, you should make a notation about that, too. One of my colleagues frequently arranges to meet friends for lunch, carefully notes the appointment in his calendar, and then, inevitably, has to call back to find out where they are meeting!

DON'T LOSE YOUR NOTES

Once you have written a list or note that reinforces your internal memory, you have to decide what to do with it. That is not always a simple decision. A note can help you remember, but it's useless as a recall aid if you cannot find it.

Some notes have obvious, logical places. A grocery list belongs in the kitchen and your list of items needed from the hardware store belongs by the workbench. Other notes, those that refer to non-routine events or errands, must be placed where you will notice them. To remember to do something before you leave the house the next morning, you could put your reminder note on the door you usually use, so you won't leave without finishing your task. Many people use a calendar for such reminders because they look at it each day. You could also use a memory place (memory places will be discussed in the following section).

Organizing the Environment

The organization of your environment can be a definite aid to your memory. Keeping things in their proper place substantially reduces the memory demands of daily life; you can save your memory power for something more important than trying to recall where the scissors are. You will also find it helpful to establish certain areas in your home and elsewhere—memory places—where you consistently put reminders and items that could otherwise be mislaid.

A PLACE FOR EVERYTHING

Organizing your possessions is essential to memory maintenance. Many people think they are losing their memory because they can never find anything. The real problem is that they are poorly organized. When they want a ruler, they mutter to themselves as they search, "Now, where was I when I last used that?" When they want to find the knife sharpener, they hunt through the kitchen cupboards. When the holiday season rolls around, the search is on for the wrapping paper.

You will save a great deal of time and mental effort by living in a well-organized house. Make it a habit to establish a specific place for everything and always return objects to their proper places. This takes time, but considerably less than repeated searches would take. Moreover, as you get older, or when you are under stress, you may not have the energy or physical mobility to look all over the house for everyday objects.

Moving. When you move to a new home or new office, you have to reorganize your belongings. For a while after the move, it takes effort to find the silverware, towels, or memo pads, things that you didn't have to think about before. Rather than risk memory overload, give yourself extra time before beginning projects that have heavy memory demands. After you learn how your things are organized, your mind will seem to work better.

MEMORY PLACES

Using a memory place adds another type of organization to your environment. You should have two memory places in your home, one for objects you need to locate every day, and the other for information or items that you use regularly, but not daily.

Wandering around several times a day looking for your reading glasses can be time-consuming and annoying. The longer you look, the more convinced you are that your memory is failing. So place glasses and other everyday articles (purse or wallet, briefcase, keys) in one location. Use a table by the door, your nightstand, or your desk. (In the office, the "in" box serves as the memory place for work that requires daily attention.)

A major benefit of having an everyday memory place is that it gives you a sure way to remember to make a phone call, give someone a message, or write a letter. If you put a reminder note in your memory place, you will see it in the morning when you pick up your things.

The second memory place is used for important business or financial items, such as bills, credit card receipts, copies of medical bills to send to the insurance company, address book, schedules, and so on. In the office, this second location (usually a bulletin board) contains notices about upcoming meetings, conferences, audits, or inspections. This is important and valuable information that only needs to be checked at regular intervals, not daily.

Just as with the everyday memory place, the advantage of this second place is that it gives you a system for remembering. Once you develop the habit of checking it regularly, you can put your list of family birthdates there, and you won't forget to buy cards. Keep the airplane tickets there for next month's trip.

Away from home. The memory place concept can be used when you are away from home as well. It's easy to forget where you have put things in a new environment and have a new routine or no routine at all. Therefore, upon your arrival at someone else's home or at your hotel room, you need to establish a memory place for your glasses, watch, and so forth. Then you won't have to search for things and you won't risk leaving anything behind.

You can also establish a memory place when you go out, to avoid forgetting an umbrella, hat, or briefcase. Usually, at a restaurant or at a meeting, you can use the area underneath and/or to the side of your chair. If you are right-handed, use the right side of your chair and say to yourself: MY THINGS WILL BE RIGHT WHERE I PUT THEM. If you are left-handed, use the left side of your chair and say: MY THINGS WILL BE WHERE I LEFT THEM. Once you establish this habit, you will never have to raceback to find some forgotten, treasured possession.

There will be times, of course, when there is no convenient memory place. At a party where people are standing or moving from place to place during the evening, put your belongings to the right (or left) of the first chair you see when you walk in the room. Upon leaving, you will notice this chair again and pick up your possessions. To remember that you hung your coat in a closet, you will have to use an internal strategy such as mental imagery. Picture yourself facing the door, which is "wearing" an oversized coat. When you see the door to leave, the image will come back to you.

Using Object Cues

The use of object cues is probably the most common memory strategy in everyday life. Timers, strings around the finger, alarm clocks, and photographs are all examples of object cues. Each one of them serves as a retrieval cue for something you want to remember. Object cues are more effective when they are specific, but general cues can also be helpful.

GENERAL OBJECT CUES

The kitchen timer—essential for the cook—is an example of a general cue; it cues you to do something without specifying what it is. Other general cues, such as turning your ring backwards or wearing your watch on the opposite wrist, also tell you that there is "something" you need to remember but do not tell you what that something is. That can be a real problem. You see the watch turned around and spend twenty minutes trying to remember why your watch has been moved.

General object cues are effective in two circumstances:

Your schedule is relatively simple. Therefore a special task will stand out in your mind.

You combine them with notes or other specific cues. The general cue tells you to look for a specific cue in your environment.

Suppose that the phone rings as you are about to go to the post office. You take the call and turn your watch around to remind you that you were interrupted. Afterward, you notice the watch and think back to what you were doing before, as you look around for a specific cue. The mail! You see it on your desk and remember to go to the post office.

Similarly, you can turn your ring around to remind you to check your appointment book, where you have recorded more specific information.

Remember to phone someone right after dinner by using a general reminder (an alarm clock) and leaving a note in your memory place.

Sharing the timer. If you use a general cue such as a timer for only one purpose, such as to remind you to turn off the stove, you will rarely have problems with the general nature of the cue. But what if you have three things cooking and cannot remember which one needs to be checked? What do you do when you are baking and watering the lawn at the same time, and the timer rings; do you turn off the oven or move the hose? The solution is to move the timer around so it is closest to whatever needs checking next.

If you use your wristwatch alarm as a timing device, be sure you don't get confused about the purpose of each alarm. Since you cannot move your watch to different locations, you need to rehearse some internal associations between times and tasks, or put a note in your everyday memory place to tell you what the alarm is for.

SPECIFIC OBJECT CUES

Cues that use specific objects are probably the most common and practical way to remember to complete actions. For example, you may lay the hammer on the kitchen table to remember to put up a painting in the den. A brown paper sack hanging from the refrigerator door reminds you to make yourself a lunch for tomorrow's meeting.

ENVIRONMENTAL CUES

A familiar environment is a powerful memory aid. Specific and general cues are all around us in our normal surroundings. You see a picture of the grandchildren and remember to call with graduation congratulations. The bills on your desk speak for themselves.

Moving to a new home may create temporary memory problems because of cue loss. If you can take most of your personal belongings with you, you will have an easier time remembering. In selecting what to leave behind, consider the memory value of your belongings. Even something as simple as a photo of an old friend (who you aren't even close to anymore) may always be a reminder to mail family birthday cards.

RETENTION STRATEGIES

Most of the time, external strategies serve you well for learning and retention. Lists can be kept for as long as you need them. The notes on your calendar eliminate the need to store information mentally. Photocopies of important letters and photographs of your family can be saved indefinitely.

But when you use internal methods for learning or when retrieval conditions require that you remember something without referring to notes, you also need internal retention strategies.

Rehearsal

When you want to retain what you have learned for a long time, you have to review and rehearse. By rehearse, I do not mean just using rote repetition, that is, saying the speech or reading the manual over and over again. Rehearsal as a retention strategy includes these steps:

Review the strategy you applied.

Rehearse your mnemonic.

Rehearse your mnemonic with the information you learned.

Using the peg system as an example, rehearsal would mean going through the same steps you did at learning and asking yourself whether your images are still good ones. Make alterations as needed. Any images that are not clear in your mind should be made more detailed or vivid.

If your strategy was to create associations to link items in a list, but your review indicates that some of those associations take a long time to recall, try to think of alternatives.

When you are satisfied that you now have a good strategy, look over the information you learned and rehearse your internal mnemonic. Both the mnemonic and the original information should be rehearsed to ensure that your mnemonic will automatically help you recall. Check that object cues or notes are still available.

Think back to the example earlier in this chapter of remembering last-minute details for your vacation trip.

You said to yourself: ANIMALS—2, HOUSE—2, PACKING—2 BY 2, AND POSSESSIONS—3.

Your primary retention strategy is to repeat this mnemonic to yourself a number of times. At intervals, you must also practice the link between it and the actual items in each category: ANIMALS—2 MEANS DOG AND CAT.

Otherwise, you won't remember the items, and the mnemonic will be useless.

Overlearning. A strong benefit of rehearsal is that it leads to overlearning, which promotes long-term retention. Overlearning occurs whenever you continue to rehearse information that has already been learned.

Distributed Practice

When should you rehearse? There is definite evidence that distributed practice—practice spread over several different sessions—is better than one long session. It is more effective to rehearse a speech for three periods of twenty minutes each than for one sixty minute session.

There are several possible reasons why distributed practice is effective:

1. You come to each session with slightly different experiences. The way you feel on Tuesday may help you think of some associations or cues you did not consider on Monday.

2. Consciously or unconsciously, when you distribute your practice over several days, you rehearse the information between study sessions.

3. Each time you approach a new study session you have some information saved or retained from the last session. In the second session you overlearn the material learned in the first. Your mnemonic gets more rehearsal, which increases the likelihood that you will remember it.

To overcome difficulties in memorizing and remembering new information, shorten the time interval between study periods to one-half day or even just a few hours. Once you find that you remember the material two hours after reviewing it, you can extend the interval gradually, until you can retain your new learning for as long as needed. Gradually increase the time until the final interval between rehearsals is the same as the length of time you will have between your last review and actual recall "test."

If you are making a presentation on Tuesday at 3:00 and the last time you will be able to study your notes is at 11:00 that morning, you will need to be able to retain your memorized speech for four hours. So the last few rehearsals should be at least four hours apart.

RECALL STRATEGIES

Reinstate Learning Conditions

You will succeed in recall by reinstating your learning conditions as much as possible, whether or not you were deliberately trying to learn. For intentional learning, think back to your mnemonic. For incidental learning, try to recall anything you may have noticed when you were first exposed to the information.

STRATEGIES

Bring to mind the images, associations, and categories you used during learning and work back from these to the original information you once learned.

If you used the peg system, try to visualize each peg in turn with its associated object.

If you used letter associations, go through the alphabet and see if a specific letter seems familiar. Frequently, when you can recall the first letter, a whole word or title will come back to you.

Don't minimize the value of external cues. In trying to recall an event from your past, look through old letters and photographs. If you believe that you may have written some information down, think about where you would put your note if you wrote it today.

Any time you can recall or locate the original learning cues and associations, you have a better chance of recalling the information you learned with those cues.

MOOD OR PHYSICAL STATE

You may have noticed that during times of sadness, sad events from your past come back into your mind. There is a relationship between your mood during learning and the mood in which you are most likely to recall what you learned. Even though it seems strange, if you were angry when you learned something, you will be more likely to recall it when you are angry again.

Having the same physical state during learning and recall can also work to your advantage. Do relaxation exercises right before studying for a test and again right before taking it, so that your physical state will be the same.

ENVIRONMENTAL CONTEXT

Any time there is a match between the environmental conditions during learning and during recall, remembering is easier. For example, to remember the names of people in your office building, don't study a list of their names at home. Take the list to your office and study it in the environment where you are used to seeing these people.

Your memories for your past life will always be recalled better in your own home than in strange or new environments. Since you cannot always return to the same context, try to imagine yourself there. You have probably used the technique before in this situation:

You walk into a room and then can't remember why you went there. You may remember by thinking about where you just were and what you were doing right before you decided to go to that room.

Thinking back to the original context can help you remember something that you did not attempt to learn when you were first exposed to it.

You and some friends are having dinner together. During the evening the stock market is discussed. You find the topic interesting, but don't pay close attention because you do not intend to invest in new stocks in the near future. The next week you change your mind, but you can't recall your friends' opinions about certain stocks.

To remember, think about how you felt that evening, who was there, what food you ate, what other topics you discussed. You may discover that you "learned" quite a bit incidentally.

Test Yourself

Self-testing has two primary benefits as a retrieval aid. First, it forces you to review the most important parts of what you have learned. Second, it gives you recall practice. If your memory search fails, you know that you need to relearn the material.

SELECTIVE TESTING

With the best form of self-testing, called selective testing, you alternate between testing yourself on all the material you have learned, and testing yourself only on those parts that you cannot remember easily.

As you practice a speech, try to say the entire speech, noting the parts you had difficulty remembering. Then study those parts and test yourself only on them. The next time, try to say the entire speech again. Selective testing provides more review to the sections that need it most.

Search Processes

Searching seems to take place automatically most of the time; you are rarely aware of it unless it fails. You may decide to recall the strategies in this chapter. If your search is successful, you think of many strategies right away. You will be aware of searching only when you cannot think of a strategy or you feel as if it is "on the tip of your tongue."

When you have a tip-of-the-tongue experience, you "know" that you know something about the information you are trying to recall. You may remember the first letter but not the entire word. You may remember someone's occupation but not his company's name. You may remember the beginning of a joke but not the punch line. Sometimes the word you were seeking pops into your head later (sometimes in the middle of the night!). It is almost as if your mind unconsciously continues to work on the problem.

TRUST YOUR INTUITION

Most people are fairly accurate in judging whether they once knew or learned a piece of information. When you sense that you never knew something, don't waste time searching your memory. Any time you do feel that you know the answer to a question, search for it and be systematic in your search.

The following search methods—based on trying to think of a word for a crossword puzzle—will help the appropriate associations work through your mind:

Think about related terms or concepts.

Think back to the last time you may have used it.

Search through the alphabet in hopes of identifying the first letter.

Reinstate the situation in which you learned the word.

WAYS TO OVERCOME BLOCKING

When you have a feeling of knowing, and the wrong information seems to come to mind, it is called blocking. You can sometimes overcome blocks by shifting your attention from the specific information you want to recall to related or associated items.

Continuing to search with the same question in mind—"What is the name of the store?"—as you try to remember the name of a company (from which you purchased an item), will keep producing the same wrong information because your search is the same. The best thing to do when you block on a name is to stop focusing on the name. Instead, try to remember when you made the purchase, how much it cost, how you learned about the company or the product. These alternative questions can bring to mind other associations that may be closely linked to the name in your mind and can help you recall it.

OTHER RECOMMENDATIONS

Multiple Strategies

Never hesitate to use multiple strategies. I have provided many examples in which two different methods were combined into one more powerful memory tool. Strategy combinations are powerful memory devices. The more methods you use, the more likely you are to remember.

You have names of several companies to remember. Note the *first letter* of each one: IBM, Apple, AT&T, NCR, and Xerox, and use *elaboration* to create a memorable word: (M) A N I A X. *Imagine* yourself running from company to company like a maniac.

You get directions to someone's house. *Listen carefully* note the *number* and *order* of right and left turns, and *write* everything down.

You have to describe a new product for a sales talk. *Outline* the main functions and new features and then *visualize* the product at work, highlighting those features in your image.

You have to remember, later in the day, to bring in your shirt from the clothes line. Use a general *object cue* such as turning your watch around, and back it up by writing yourself a *note* that you put in your everyday *memory place*.

Suit the Strategy to the Task

The strategy you select should fit the type of material you want to remember. Unless you want to start pulling groceries off your kitchen shelves, specific object cues will not be very useful for recalling a grocery list. Use a written list or an internal list using the method of loci, verbal elaboration, the peg system, or interactive imagery. You would have a hard time recalling abstract art, fabric samples, or blueprints with verbal elaborations. Instead, use imagery.

Consider both the learning and recall situations in selecting your strategy. Some hair stylists and insurance salesmen are very impressive in their ability to recall details about their clients. They don't write notes in the presence of the client because that would be disruptive, so they use internal methods such as association and imagery. They may write notes later. Before their next appointment with the client, they review their notes and remember the information internally again, using the same strategies as before. Then they can ask about the client's research, investments, vacation plans, or children. Their particular combination of internal and external methods is selected to suit their specific learning and recall requirements.

Develop Routines

Do you forget tasks that you have to do on a regular basis? One very useful memory technique is to make these part of a regular routine. The value of routines is that you can usually carry them out without very much conscious effort or attention. Until the routines are established, though, you'll need to pay attention and concentrate on your actions.

Gary used to alternately overwater or underwater his plants. He just watered when he happened to notice them and, of course, they weren't very healthy. Finally turning his attention to the problem, he decided that he could remember to water the plants by making it part of his weekly laundry routine. He associated the plant "washing" with the clothes washing. Watering the plants became part of his established pattern of behavior.

What to Do Now

Make the effort to maximize your memory power. If you follow these recommendations, your memory will probably improve even if you don't master mental imagery or verbal elaboration:

Choose strategies that fit your memory skills and requirements.
Associate new information with familiar information.
Develop distinctive, meaningful images and verbal elaborations.
Organize written materials you want to learn.
Use external aids and your best internal strategies as backups.
Use specific notes and cues.
Organize your home and/or office.
Combine strategies when you can.
Search systematically, keeping in mind known associations.
Code or reorganize information into the shortest mnemonic that will help retrieve the original information.
Rehearse and self-test repeatedly.
Reinstate learning conditions during recall.

Any time you approach memory tasks with the attitude that a strategy should be used, and you work to apply a strategy, chances are you will remember a great deal even if you were unable to create a distinctive image or clever elaboration. Your involvement with the information will be greatly increased—you'll spend more time thinking about it and more associations will occur to you. That in itself will improve your recall.

8

Attention and Memory

Do you function on automatic pilot most of the day?
If you are interrupted, do you forget what you were doing?
Is it difficult to concentrate on conversations or on reading?
Are you easily distracted?
In other words, are your memory failures really attention failures?
If the answer is yes, you need to start paying attention now!

Paying attention is the first step to successful remembering.
Simply by attending to information, you enter it into short-term
memory storage. To retain information in long-term memory, you
need to first pay attention and then use learning strategies.

People commonly "turn off" their minds when they are tending
to normal, routine activities. As you get older you may have a
tendency to do this more than you used to. Instead of allowing long

periods of absent-mindedness to occur, you should take note of what you are doing, seeing, and hearing.

Attention is normally selective—that is, you attend to part of the world and ignore the rest. Sometimes, however, you may find yourself unable to concentrate exclusively on the task or information of your choosing because you are distracted. That, too, becomes more common as a person gets older. Therefore, you must eliminate the distractions and find ways to focus your attention.

LACK OF ATTENTION

Potential Problems

ROUTINE

William James, one of the first modern psychologists, wrote in 1890: "Habit diminishes the conscious attention with which our acts are performed."

Being a creature of habit can cause embarrassment, inconvenience, or real danger. If, for example, the last part of your dressing routine is to change from slippers to street shoes, you could leave the house in your slippers by not paying attention when your routine is interrupted. If you follow the same route to work each day, your car may "take you" to work on weekends. If you always turn off the oven immediately upon removing the pan, you probably do it without thinking. A distraction could make you forget to turn it off. The result could be a burnt oven or even a fire.

Your way of doing things can become so ingrained that important responsibilities can be forgotten.

Henry is a productive and competent professor who usually "tunes out" his job on weekends and enjoys his family. One Sunday he completely forgot he had promised to give a speech to the Over 50 Club. He obviously failed to give special attention to this obligation. He had proceeded with the "weekend as usual" until the organization president phoned to ask where he was. Henry was embarrassed. He also lost some credibility with this group.

AUTOMATIC PILOT

Ask yourself if most of your time is spent in activities that are highly similar from one day to the next. Do you eat the same breakfast and lunch at the same times? Do you read the newspaper in the morning, go to the grocery story in the afternoon, and watch the news on TV at night?

If many of your activities are carried out in an identical manner day after day, you are probably not using your mind much. You are operating on "automatic pilot," not totally aware of what you are doing, not alert, and not paying attention to your surroundings. In this condition—a form of highway hypnosis—you can easily forget where you have put things, forget what you were about to do, or forget whether or not you have done something already. This can happen to people living highly scheduled lives in institutions, but it should not happen to people living independently.

If you frequently function on automatic pilot, you may have forgotten what it is like to attend to new information or keep track of what you are doing. Your attentional skills, and consequently your memory power, may even deteriorate.

In a new situation, especially, you may find it difficult to deal with anything that is not routine. If a street that you normally take to work is closed for construction, you can forget to take an alternate route when you leave home in the morning. If you move, you may automatically reach for the phone as if it were located where it was in your previous home. New environments require extra attentiveness, and weakened attention skills may make it harder to adjust.

EVERYDAY ACTIVITIES

Ordinary daily events are easy to forget because they do not stand out in your mind. You don't recall that you picked up the newspaper because there's nothing memorable about it. You have dinner in a restaurant you've been to before and there is nothing to notice or remember. But if the waiter spills a glass of water on you, you'll probably stew about it for hours and, as a result, remember that meal. Of course, if this kind of mishap occurs every time you eat out, it will no longer be unusual and it will not receive any special attention.

Much of your memory for daily events and activities, whether routine or not, is incidental memory—that is, you make no effort to remember at the time. You don't work to remember yesterday's breakfast or where you placed a magazine. Successful incidental memory depends upon attention, which means that you will not retain much about your life if you are not alert to your surroundings.

How to Increase Attentiveness

There are several ways that you can increase your general attentiveness:

Become more observant.

Practice paying attention to everyday behavior.

Prevent interruptions from causing memory failure.

BECOME MORE OBSERVANT

If you were walking through a shopping mall and wanted people to pay attention to you, what would you do? You would probably apply a basic principle of attention-getting—you would try to stand out. With this in mind, you might wear bright, colorful clothing. Speak or sing loudly. Act strangely. Stand on a tall soapbox. Jump up and down.

To capture *your* attention, information or events need to stand out in your mind. If something is not bright, loud, unusual, large, moving, or otherwise memorable, you need to make it noticeable in some other way. When something is distinctive it stands out against a general background and naturally receives more attention, whether or not you intend to remember it.

Each activity, book, person, assignment, or letter will become more distinctive if you become aware of its special properties. In other words, you must become more observant.

How to improve observation. How observant are you? Without looking at them, try to draw accurate pictures of some common objects: a penny or dime, the front of your telephone, an American flag. Unless you are a keen observer, your recall will not be highly accurate. But you can improve your powers of observation with practice. Begin by noticing details in your surroundings. Look at the pictures on your walls and then try to describe them.

Try this exercise. Open a book with photographs and study one picture, then close the book and try to list the features in that picture. With a photo of a person, see if you can remember clothing and hair style, eye color, the shape of the nose, and the background. Pretend you are going to draw a caricature and decide what facial characteristics you would emphasize. With a photo of trees, notice the shape and color of the leaves, the number and orientation of the branches, the appearance of clouds in the sky, and the details of shadows cast by the trees. Now open the book and find two details you missed before. Continue checking the picture for missed details until you are convinced that you have noticed everything.

With practice, you should soon see a change in your observation powers. You will notice more and more at first glance. Pictures that once seemed to be similar will become distinct because each nuance of color and shape will attract your interest. As you learn to observe the distinctive features of objects, events, and people, your overall attentiveness will improve, and everything you encounter will be more memorable.

Benefits in daily life. Keen observation can help you recall whether or not you have completed daily tasks, such as unplugging the iron or taking out the garbage. Do you ever get into bed at night and then wonder whether or not you have locked the door? Even if you remember turning the latch, you still aren't sure if you are remembering that night or the night before!

To overcome this kind of problem, identify something unique about this event each day. One night you might count the lights in the neighbors' windows. Another night you might notice where your dog is sleeping as you approach the door. You could walk by the hall mirror after locking the door and note what you are wearing. By associating a special observation with this everyday action, you can keep it from being entirely routine.

PRACTICE PAYING ATTENTION TO YOUR BEHAVIOR

I recommend that you analyze automatic behaviors and habits that you typically ignore. You will benefit in two ways: your mind will be kept alert (off automatic pilot), and you will gain practice paying attention.

Start with something simple. Ask yourself questions about your everyday actions. Which hand do you use to turn on the light switch in the bathroom? to remove your glasses? to pick up your purse or wallet? Do you take the same route to work each day? Describe that route. How do you place your glasses when you put them down? Do you get dressed in the same order each day? Try to list that order.

Now take note of what you are doing every time you carry out a habitual daily activity. Become aware of the number of steps taken or the amount of time. You could make this exercise meaningful by thinking about ways to shorten the task or reduce your effort. For example, if you discover that the placement of clothing in your drawers requires you to use extra effort in getting dressed, you could rearrange the drawers. The point of the exercise is not to simplify your life, but to get your mind working while you carry out routine or ordinary actions, and not let it wander.

You could go one step further and try to change some of your routines. You would thus force yourself to avoid automatic pilot and practice self-attentiveness with a goal in mind. You could use the same technique for ridding yourself of a bad habit.

Changing automatic behavior. To change behavior that is automatic, you will need to pay close attention and monitor yourself. Write yourself notes to remind you of your goal. Put it on your calendar. Ask someone else to remind you. I'm sure your spouse, children, or employer will be more than willing to help you change a "bad" habit. Select a substitute for your habit and focus your attention on this alternative. Keep a checklist to indicate how often you carried out your old habit and your new behavior.

For further encouragement, offer yourself a reward for success. If you can substantially reduce the number of times that you absent-mindedly perform your old habit, have a special dessert, go out to dinner, or buy yourself a gift.

PAY ATTENTION IN SPITE OF INTERRUPTIONS

An interruption can easily make you forget what you were doing; this is true for both habitual and non-habitual behavior. You forget what you were doing because the interruption grabs your attention. That is how immediate memory works—forgetting occurs because new information displaces the earlier thoughts.

What you can do. Because of the nature of immediate memory, one way to get back to the task after an interruption is to "hold your place" mentally. In other words, you must find a way to maintain attention to the original task and keep it in mind while carrying out the activity that caused the interruption.

As the mother of two young children, much of my life revolves around the kitchen/playroom area. If I am cooking when the phone rings, I can say over and over to myself, "I need to go back to the stove after this phone call . . . I am working on dinner . . . I still have one course to go." The effectiveness of this tactic depends on the nature of the interruption. When I get an important business call, I need to concentrate all my mental energy on it, and, as a result, I tend to forget what I was doing.

Another useful method for returning to your task after an interruption is to identify an object to use as a cue. I use the kitchen timer. When I am interrupted, I simply pick up the timer and hold it in my hand. After dealing with the distraction, I am reminded by the timer that I was doing something earlier. Any object can serve as a cue as long as it's easy to hold and located in a convenient place. Some people move a ring to the wrong finger or turn a watch backwards; their hand does not feel right with the object out of place and it cues them to remember.

You might, alternatively, write yourself a note and put it in your memory place. Or, if someone else is working with you, you could ask that person to remind you to return to your "place" after the interruption.

Benefits of Increasing Attentiveness

When you are attentive to your behavior and to your environment, you are unlikely to encounter many of the memory problems described in this chapter. You will find it easier to learn, retain, and recall. By staying alert, you have a good chance of recalling details about past events that you did not learn intentionally.

On automatic pilot, you are not using your mind very much. In a sense, then, enhanced attentiveness is an important step toward maintaining minimum intellectual stimulation. By being observant, you may see or hear things that excite your curiosity.

Increased attentiveness can help you adjust to minor alterations in routine. You are more likely to remember to stop at the dry cleaners on your way home from work if you have previously analyzed your routine. Knowing your usual route, you can identify the best place to make a detour and set up a memory strategy so you won't absent-mindedly go straight home.

Paying more attention to your behavior can aid your adjustment when major changes in habit or routine are required, as after a move or a job change. This type of change demands attention and memory effort, but you will find it easier if you have analyzed your habitual behaviors and have practiced using memory strategies to modify habits.

Sometimes an accident or illness will force a change in your routine.

Jim realized that he had been going upstairs to see the central office secretary four or five times each day, taking care of one task at a time. Although it was inefficient, it was no problem for him. But when he sprained his ankle playing soccer, he had to modify his routine. Fortunately, Jim had already observed this pattern of behavior and was able to use memory aids to review the entire day's work and then make only one trip upstairs.

Automatic pilot is necessary. Although you clearly benefit from paying more attention to everything you do, I am not suggesting that you should never do anything automatically.

You could not function effectively without automatic pilot. You drive to work without noticing every turn, you recognize familiar faces in the hall without analyzing the person's features, you type automatically. Automatic activities take less thinking, less attention, less mental energy, and less time. They can be very beneficial. The danger occurs when you lose your attention skills and operate on automatic pilot too much of the time.

LACK OF CONCENTRATION

Closely allied with attention is concentration. Concentration is essential to memory success, whether you want to remember the employment policies of your company, a presentation to a client, a new language, a new diet, a list of names, or instructions for medications. An increased ability to concentrate will ensure that you can accomplish all kinds of tasks in a reasonable amount of time. Along with increased concentration skill, your efficiency will improve dramatically.

Potential Problems

If you cannot focus your attention, you will take more time to learn new information or you may not learn it at all. When you want to recall something you already know, you may find that you have not retained more than the gist of it. The details escape you.

EXTERNAL DISTRACTIONS

As you get older, concentration problems are more likely to occur because of heightened distractibility. You cannot recall the names of the people you met at a party because there was a lot of commotion in the room and you hardly noticed the names in the first place. You're not sure what a friend said about his vacation plans because there was a news broadcast on the radio while he was talking.

Unless you live by yourself in a quiet neighborhood or work in a quiet office, you will find your memory constantly affected by outside noises and interruptions. You could read an entire chapter in a book, only to discover you had completely lost track of the plot.

INTERNAL DISTRACTIONS

Intrusive thoughts and daydreams can prevent you from remembering what you have read or heard.

Daniel is an attorney who recently had to handle a complex child custody case. It was important for him to complete the work quickly, but every time he tried to recall the facts and the arguments he wanted to make, he found himself lost in personal wonderings about his own marital problems and children. As a result, Daniel took more than twice as long as he should have to finish preparing for the case.

Internal distractions such as Daniel's can lead to overload because you don't finish your memory tasks, and your responsibilities accumulate. Overload can also occur if new responsibilities overwhelm you. Whatever the reason, once your memory becomes overloaded, concentration becomes even more difficult. Symptoms of overload may include an inability to complete one mental task before another comes along, and a constant racing of your mind from one idea to the next.

Nancy is an active volunteer. She agreed to arrange the annual bazaar for her club and had asked several people to chair committees, but she could not remember who had agreed to serve or on which committees. Remembering phone conversations is something Nancy normally does easily, but in this case, every time she tried to remember previous phone calls, she began to think about other arrangements that needed to be made. There were too many things on her mind, and ultimately she had to call everyone again.

MOTIVATION

Motivation is related to concentration. When you are motivated to remember something, it will readily attract your attention even though you may not be aware of your attentional effort.

Your motivation to have a flourishing garden will guarantee that you pay attention to your neighbor with the green thumb as he tells you what he does in his garden. Without that motivation, you won't remember when or where to plant the tomatoes.

When the head of personnel is rattling on about a problem he's mentioned ten other times, you do not feel the need to listen, and you begin to mentally review ways to increase sales. Suddenly you notice that he's changed the topic but you have no idea what he has said to you.

HEALTH

Concentration may be difficult when you are tired or ill. In most cases this is a fleeting problem, and you should not exaggerate its importance. If your concentration skills are generally good, they will return. If they are not very good, try to improve them.

How to Improve Concentration

Selective attention is the key to good concentration. Two recommendations I made earlier in the chapter apply here:

Make things you want to remember more distinctive so they will stand out.

Make sure that you don't lose your place after interruptions.

In addition, you should eliminate distractions, set deadlines, establish a concentration period, establish priorities, and increase motivation.

CAPTURE YOUR ATTENTION

One way to make written information distinctive is to mark it with a bright color or write it in large letters. Students use colorful highlighting pens to mark important phrases in their textbooks. If you want to memorize the key points from a report, write them in large, red letters on flash cards.

HOLD YOUR PLACE DURING INTERRUPTIONS

When you want to remember material you are reading or studying, you need to remain task oriented in spite of interruptions. Hold your place in your mind or use a cue to ensure that you return to the memory work after a disruption. If you find it difficult to regain your train of thought, get in the habit of jotting down some quick notes and marking your place whenever you are interrupted.

ELIMINATE DISTRACTIONS

Whether distractions are external or internal, you have to systematically identify them and then eliminate them. In a sense, they put you into a divided attention situation that is likely to reduce your ability to remember what you want to.

External distractions. You can deal with external distractions by defining your memory objective and then determining what in the environment is relevant to your goal and what should be ignored. If you are reading *The Wall Street Journal* to learn about the impact of proposed tax changes, don't break your concentration by reading stories about commodities. No matter how interesting they may be, they distract you from your main purpose.

Remove or close yourself off from objects, sounds, stories, or sights that continue to distract you even though you know you should ignore them. There is no point in trying to remember something when you cannot give it your full attention. Close the door so you won't hear the kids. Does the television keep you from concentrating on your reading? Turn it off. Do you find yourself staring at the trees outside the window? Get curtains (you can enjoy nature after you are finished). Clear your desk of papers unrelated to the project you're working on. When you find yourself flipping through a journal to irrelevant articles, cut out the pages you need to read and put away the journal.

On the other hand, you don't need to eliminate something that does not capture your attention. Many teenagers can study with rock music blaring in their ears because they don't pay any attention to it.

Internal distractions. You have to rid yourself of distracting ideas and get back to the work at hand, or nothing will get accomplished. Internal distractions require a different kind of elimination tactic than external distractions.

Do you have miscellaneous ideas bombarding your brain? You must find a quick way to rid yourself of them. Sometimes you can get them off your mind for the time being by writing them down. Or you may need to take a short break to develop them, if you are feeling especially creative on the wrong topic.

Sometimes ideas flit by rapidly and you are unable to focus on any of them. You may have associations related to the material you want to learn mixed in with other, disruptive ideas. You need to slow down your mind so that you can "catch" your important thoughts. It may help you to relax by taking deep breaths for several minutes, focusing on your breathing. Imagine yourself at a very relaxing place, such as a beach, a forest, or a mountain top. Stay away from coffee if it makes your thoughts race.

If none of the above methods help you concentrate better, try using "task-directed internal speech." This simply means talking yourself through a complex task as a way of keeping track of what you are doing.

Task-directed internal speech. Begin by stating—out loud—a series of task-directed questions or comments, and answer them:

First I decide what I want to remember.
I want to remember what the tax manual says about self-employment.
How many parts does it have?
It has four headings.
Which part am I going to learn first?
Concentrate first on the reporting requirements.
Choose a memory strategy.
The best strategy for me to learn these instructions is the PQRST method.

Have I selected a strategy I can use effectively?
Yes.

After you have made a strategy decision, talk yourself through the memory task. Identify the steps you need to do and evaluate your progress.

Do the first step in the strategy.
First I have to preview the whole article by reading it through quickly.
Follow with the next step.
Then I decide what questions I need to be able to answer. Let's see, the questions will be: What criteria do I use to define work as self-employment? What deductions can I make? What forms do I need to fill out? What records do I need to keep?
How am I doing?
I am following the strategy carefully; I have completed the first two steps.
Do the next step.
Now I should state the gist of what I have read.
How am I doing?

Self-instructions normally begin as vocalized statements. Gradually say them more and more quietly until they become internal speech. If your internal speech is task-directed, it will not be distracting.

SET DEADLINES

Set a deadline for completing each memory task. If you need to memorize a piece of music for a concert, an after-dinner speech for the Rotary Club, or 100 vocabulary words for your language class, you can focus your attention better by establishing a deadline and working toward it.

In setting a deadline, try to make a realistic assessment of how much time you need to complete your task. (Over the years I have discovered that it takes me twice as long to memorize something as I thought it would.) A complex memory task can be made easier by separating it into parts and deciding on several interim deadlines.

ESTABLISH A CONCENTRATION PERIOD

Your concentration period is the amount of time you can sustain effective mental effort. To determine your ideal time period on a memorizing task, monitor yourself.

Set a timer for thirty minutes. If you find yourself daydreaming when it rings, you know that you have allowed your attention to wander. Keep a tally of the number of times that you notice yourself thinking about something else. Note how much you can recall.

Experiment with different time periods to determine the best length for you. Some people find that a short study period forces them to pay attention right away, and others find that a short period doesn't work at all because they tend to think about the next thing they have to do. Select the concentration period that results in the lowest number of daydreaming incidents and the highest recall.

ESTABLISH PRIORITIES

Determine your priorities and plan to accomplish each memory activity in turn. Priority setting is especially useful when you are overloaded, but it can be beneficial even when you are not. If you are overloaded, try to delegate some responsibilities.

Priority decisions may be difficult, but they can improve your ability to concentrate because you won't need to think about items near the bottom of the list. Setting a goal to complete one task at a time clears your mind; it is less likely to be jumbled up with miscellaneous memories and associations related to multiple obligations.

How to establish priorities. You may have three memory tasks that require concentrated effort:

Update your calendar with the appointments you arranged when you were away from your desk yesterday (this is urgent).

Memorize the details of three case studies you want to use during the week.

Write a summary of twenty research reports to submit to a periodical next month.

Start by separating each of these into subparts that can be done independently. In this instance it makes sense to order the tasks in terms of due dates, but you could also put things that most interest you at the top of your priority list. As you put these tasks in order, note the level of concentration required by each:

Priority 1. Update calendar (level of concentration: low)

Priority 2. Review case studies one at a time (low)

Priority 3. Reread the five research reports that you do not recall clearly (high)

Priority 4. Begin to write research summary (high)

Priority 5. Reread all research reports and compare authors' conclusions with your summary (low).

When you are ready, sit down with your timer and the first priority job, eliminate distractions, and get to work. Work for the full length of your concentration period. If you finish before the time is up, begin the next task. After the time interval is over, take a break. If you haven't completed the second task, return to it after resting.

Your list should be regarded as a guideline and not a law. If you have been working on an activity that requires high concentration, and you feel too "burnt out" to make a substantial effort again after a break, shift to a low concentration activity for the next time period, even if that means that you change the order.

The top item may require considerable mental energy. When you are feeling under the weather, move down to the next item that you can complete with low effort. Fatigue and illness prevent high concentration, but you don't want to waste the time that you have set aside. After you have finished some of your work, you will be less anxious and therefore will concentrate better when you're well again.

All of your memory tasks will be accomplished if you work through your priority list systematically.

INCREASE MOTIVATION

Your concentration will improve when you are strongly motivated. Ideally, you could pick only fascinating topics of your own choosing. However, family or job responsibilities frequently demand that you remember many things that do not interest you. When this happens, try to increase your motivation through rewards. Promise yourself a day at the pool, for example, or an evening out when you complete the job. When internal motivation is lacking, an external reward can spur you to work harder.

Rewards with time contingencies have the strongest impact on concentration. Don't just reward yourself for studying, but give yourself a large reward for completing the memory job quickly and smaller rewards for slower performance. Test yourself to make sure that you can recall as much as needed before you give yourself the reward.

Benefits of Improving Concentration

By following these suggestions, you should be able to reduce the number of internal and external distractions and focus your mind more narrowly on specific memory tasks. Your increased efficiency will make it less likely that you will experience overload. The net result is that you should be able to learn faster and recall more.

When you increase your ability to concentrate, you ensure that you can accomplish all kinds of tasks in a reasonable amount of time. Along with increased concentration skill, your efficiency will improve dramatically.

9

How to Remember Names

When I ask people to tell me about their memory problems, their most common complaint is difficulty remembering names. At any age, this is the one everyday memory skill that few people can master. Names are difficult for two reasons:

When we meet someone new, we usually hear his name just once.

Most names do not have meaning in themselves.

Hearing the Name Once

People who have trouble remembering names often say, "I never forget a face." That is because the face is usually in front of them for a long period of time. If the name were "in front of" them for as long as the face, they would find it easier to remember the name and to match it to the face.

Lack of Meaning

Because most names do not have an intrinsic meaning, you have no way to associate them with something you already know. I am rather lucky in this respect because my first and last names are common English words. To remember my name you might say to yourself, "The robin is flying west."

Some names have meaning in another language. For example, Schwarzwald means "black forest" and Wainwright means "wagon builder." Since most of us are not proficient in many languages, one way to remember such names is to give them meaning in our own language. Anything that makes material meaningful makes it more memorable.

SIMPLE STRATEGIES

There are a number of things you can do to improve your memory for names. Some are easy; others will be more difficult to apply. Try some of the easier methods first.

Pay Attention

How often have you been introduced to someone and found that, a mere two seconds later, you cannot remember the name? Although this may seem to be an immediate memory lapse, it probably is not a memory problem at all—it is an attention problem. To increase your memory for names, *you must pay attention*. This sounds simple, but most people rarely do it.

When someone is introduced to you, listen carefully. You may not be able to "catch" the name if the introduction is given rapidly. When that happens, ask for the name to be repeated, pronounced slowly, spelled, or whatever you need to have it clearly in mind.

Learning the spelling of a name can sometimes aid your memory, and most people are flattered when you show an interest in their names. If you've taken the time to learn how to spell and pronounce the name of someone you've just met, you're well on your way to committing that name to memory.

Hearing problems. Sometimes people who have trouble hearing withdraw from social activity because their hearing problem interferes with their ability to remember names. They are embarrassed to ask people to speak slowly and clearly for them. Avoiding parties and other group functions is a mistake because social activity promotes physical health and satisfaction with life.

Don't be afraid to ask for a name to be repeated slowly and as many times as you require to be sure of it. After all, the person who introduced you may have glossed over the name because he wasn't sure about it either!

Repeat the Name

The next step is to try to keep the person's name in front of you for the entire time that his face is in front of you. Look at the person's face as he is speaking and say the name to yourself over and over. This internal rehearsal helps ensure that you will not forget the name immediately. Use the name aloud if you can.

Look for an opportunity to introduce your new acquaintance to someone else. "Miss Smith, this is Mr. Johnson." Or ask him a question: "What do you do for a living, Mr. Johnson?"

You are very likely, in your conversation, to learn something about him that will make him—and his name—more memorable. You may find some meaningful connection between his name and his occupation or hobbies. Mr. Johnson, for example, may collect memorabilia about presidents, and Johnson is the name of one of our recent presidents. Or maybe, in looking at him, you can convince yourself that he looks like a president.

Use the Names of Your Friends

Many people are embarrassed to discover that they are unable to introduce someone they have known for years and years. They just can't remember that person's name!

You see some people frequently, maybe once a week at the grocery or every few days in your office building, but you rarely use their names. Then, when you have to make an introduction, you draw a blank. Or you remember the last but not the first name.

The problem occurs because you do not use these peoples' names on a regular basis. You smile when you see your next door neighbor, you say hello to him and chat for a while, but you do not use his name. Eventually, it becomes difficult to recall, even though you know it very well (it's running around *somewhere* in your head, or it may be right on the tip of your tongue) because you do not associate his name with his face.

Therefore, do not get into the habit of ignoring names. When you see someone you know, say hello by name. Or if you feel awkward doing that, at least say the name to yourself to keep it alive in your memory. It is very embarrassing when you cannot introduce an old friend or neighbor. Believe me, I know!

Set Memory Goals

Large parties often present a problem because you meet so many new people at one time. Unless you have developed highly sophisticated techniques for remembering names (such as the image-name match technique described later in this chapter), you will do better if you set limits for yourself. Three to five names is a reasonable number. Actually, if you can learn *and remember* the names of five new people, you'll have done very well. Don't make the effort to remember any more than that. Chances are you won't succeed at learning more than five and you'll miss out on some party fun while you're thinking about all those names. It's not worth it.

Make Appearance Notes

Once you have heard a name correctly and used it once or twice, you may also wish to write it down with some identifying information.

I make appearance notes to remember the names of my students in class. I usually have a list of their names, and next to each name I put a little comment as I call the roll for the first time. I write a brief description that helps me associate each name with the person's appearance, such as "beard and glasses," "long hair, thin," "redhead." I keep the list and the notes with me until I learn everyone's name.

If you carry a date book or calendar, you could jot down people's names and appearance notes next to the notation about the event where you met them. You may think it awkward to get out a calendar and take down names at a party, but it's a lot more awkward to forget the names.

Any time a list of names is available (with club memberships, for example), appearance notes can be very effective. After each gathering, you can look over the list at home and make appearance notes next to the names you learned. Make notes that focus only on facial features, height or size, hair color and style, or other relatively permanent aspects of a person's appearance. Noting clothing or jewelry will not help because they will probably be different the next time you see the person.

Check your notes before meeting with this group the next time. Try to get mental pictures of all the people for whom you wrote notes so you can recognize them and call them by name.

Your appearance notes will be the key to remembering a person's face. If you have trouble getting these mental pictures, think back to each person and ask yourself some questions: Who introduced him to me? How long did I talk to him? What did we talk about? What was he wearing? Was he the first or the last new person I met? What kind of voice did he have? Did he tell me anything about his job, hobbies, or family? Where were we standing in the room? Any details that you can remember about the meeting place and the situation may trigger an association and bring to mind a picture of the person's face.

Even if you cannot picture the face by reviewing the notes, you can try to memorize the descriptions that go with each name. Let's say you just can't picture Lynne Warren, beside whose name you have written FRECKLES, WEARING GLASSES. But if you can memorize

"Lynne Warren—freckles and glasses," you may find a woman with freckles and glasses at the next gathering of the group. "Aha" you will say to yourself, "That woman must be Lynne Warren." You will probably remember her after that.

Whenever you have a list of people who will be attending an upcoming meeting or party, look over their names before you go to the event. You will be more likely to remember the people you meet there. If, in addition, you return home and make appearance notes (use a tape recorder if you prefer), your chances of remembering the names and faces will be even better.

COMPLEX STRATEGIES

Mental Imagery

Mental imagery means visualization, or getting a picture in your mind. People vary greatly in their ability to use this technique, but it is a skill that can be improved through practice. There is considerable evidence that people of all ages can learn to use imagery to remember faces and names.

To find out if imagery for faces comes easily for you, take a few minutes for this simple test. While watching a newscaster or entertainer on TV, try to form a mental picture of that person's face. Pick out what seems to be the most prominent feature of the person's face and focus on that. Close your eyes and look at your internal image. Is it as clear as a photograph? Can you see a definite outline of the shape of the face? Can you picture the person's hairstyle clearly? What is the facial expression? After forming the image in your mind, look back at the face and then close your eyes to put more detail into your internal image.

If you cannot create a clear mental picture for this person, try again with a face that is more familiar (yourself or a close friend). If, after several attempts, you find that you cannot get a clear picture of anyone, not even people you know very well, you may decide to choose other techniques for remembering faces and names.

Improving your ability. On the other hand, you may be motivated enough to practice the technique, which is a very useful memory tool for any kind of information. To become more proficient at translating external details into internal pictures, you will probably need to practice at least once a day for a week, using the method just described.

As soon as you can rapidly form detailed images during practice sessions, you are ready to begin using imagery to remember names with faces.

> When you meet a person, silently repeat his name while examining his face. Notice a prominent feature such as a receding hairline, a hook nose, or a double chin, and make sure that this feature is captured in your picture. You may want to exaggerate it to make it stand out in your mind. Look away briefly and see if you can form a mental picture of the face while continuing to say the name to yourself.

Even if your imagery attempt is not very successful, the effort you make to form the image will help you remember the name and face together. And the mental challenge you give yourself will keep your mind alert and flexible for learning.

Name Sentences

The name sentence technique is a form of verbal elaboration—the sentence elaborates or builds on a name to make it more meaningful.

As a first step, look for one or more meaningful words (the fewer, the better) embedded in the name, in English or any other language you know (crossword buffs and bilingual persons have an advantage here). Then put these words together in one sentence that makes sense to you. Examine the person's face and study the facial features as you try to find meaningful words, so the name and face become connected in your mind.

> The example I gave at the beginning of this chapter illustrates verbal elaboration. Do you still remember how to recall my

name? Robin West: THE ROBIN IS FLYING WEST. You can also remember:

George Beatty: WHAT A GORGEOUS BEAUTY

Frances Conner: SHE'LL HAVE A FRESH ICE CREAM CONE

Clem Walters: CLAM IN THE WATER

Alice Brady: SHE'S ALWAYS BRAIDING

Karen Boatwright: SHE'S CARRYING THE BOAT SHE MADE (a wright is a builder).

Julie Andrews: WHAT JEWELS HER HAND DREW!

It is not essential to put the parts of the name in the correct order. For Julie Andrews, you could say that her HAND DREW JEWELS or for Karen Boatwright, HER BOAT IS CAREENING TO THE RIGHT. But the name will come more readily to mind if the sentence is in the correct order.

You may think that verbal elaboration forces you to remember more information since the sentence contains more words than the name itself. Technically, that is so. But the additional words create one larger whole that makes sense. If the sentence is meaningful as a unit, it easily brings the whole name to mind.

Match Name Sentences to Appearance

Name sentences are most useful when you can connect them to the person's appearance. Silly sentences are memorable and help you recall a person's name along with his appearance. You can also have a lot of fun being creative in this way.

So instead of thinking of Clem Walters, who smiles a lot, as CLAM IN THE WATER, say HAPPY AS A CLAM IN THE WATER.

Frances Conner is not just a FRESH ICE CREAM CONE, but a FRESH VANILLA ICE CREAM CONE because her hair is white.

George Beatty is a BIG GORGEOUS BEAUTY because he is tall.

One of my memory course participants thought I had a sunny disposition, so she remembered me as RED SUNSET. Built into that short association is the sunny disposition, the "Red, Red Robin" song you may know, and the sunset in the west.

Alice Brady, of course, has long hair that she's ALWAYS BRAID-ING.

Floyd Denton, who has huge teeth, needs FLUORIDE ON HIS DENTURES.

Ken Wald wears thick glasses and CAN BUMP INTO WALLS.

To be certain you don't forget the sentence, write it on a note pad when you meet a new person and underline the relevant parts. Even if you lose your notes, just writing the sentence reinforces the name in your mind. As you continue to use the technique your speed will improve gradually. Your goal is to create name sentences quickly, during introductions if possible.

Practice at home with names of club members, school board members, movie stars, whatever. You'll be more motivated to succeed if you work with a list of names you want to learn anyway. You may surprise yourself by learning some names that you thought you would *never* remember.

The Image-Name Match Method

Now we come to the most sophisticated and complex technique for remembering names and faces. The memory experts who use it can learn hundreds of names rapidly. Basically, it involves combining two methods I've already described—imagery and name sentences. I call it the image-name match method. With mastery of this technique, the world is at your fingertips!

These are the steps:

1. Create an image of a person's face, focusing on a prominent feature.

2. Find meaningful words embedded in the name.

3. Form a new, expanded image that links the prominent feature with the meaningful words.

I usually tell my psychology students on the first day of class that they should imagine my face on the face of a bird (and I may wear a red dress to make it easy), and visualize that bird on the west end of a weather vane, with long hair flowing out behind. Thus my face and a prominent feature (long hair) dominate an image that depicts the elements in my meaningful name sentence: THE ROBIN IS FLYING WEST. Some students might consider my nose to be a prominent feature, and they could picture my "bird's beak" instead of my hair.

If you go back to the name sentences used previously, you could focus on the eyes of George Beatty: HE'D BE GORGEOUS EXCEPT FOR HIS BEADY EYES. As you imagine his face, make his eyes look like large beads.

Frances Conner may have a prominent nose that can become the ice cream cone in your image. If her hair is white, picture it as ice cream piled on top of her head. You probably won't want to tell Frances Conner that you imagine ice cream all over her head, though she might find it amusing.

You can put Clem Walters' brilliant smile on the face of a clam in the sea.

Alice Brady's hair can be the focus of your image, or if she is heavy set, you may change your name sentence to SHE'S ALWAYS BROAD-EH?" and picture her round face as you say it.

For Karen Boatwright, visualize a boat in her hair, ear, mouth, or nose, whichever is most noticeable for you.

For Julie Andrews, you could imagine her hand drawing a jewel in her mouth as she sings or you could imagine jewels stuck in her blond hair which she "draws" out with her hand.

These mental pictures may seem bizarre or absurd, but that is what makes them easy to remember. Unusual images are often the most vivid, but they do not need to be absurd to be memorable. They just need to connect the meaningful elements in the name to the most obvious features in the face, and they need to be clear and detailed. It helps to have a creative imagination.

Don't be discouraged. At first you may hardly ever think of a meaningful sentence to fit a person's name, nor will you be able to conjure up a mental picture of the face, much less put these two together. But I'm absolutely certain that this technique works.

If you make an effort to find the meaningful elements in a person's name and try to image the face with an emphasis on some prominent feature, you will probably remember the name when you see the face. It will come to mind almost automatically. Eventually you will find that creating a mental image, thinking of a name sentence, and connecting the two will become faster and easier. Don't be afraid to try. Practice using it in your everyday life with neighbors, TV personalities, and friends.

Even if you don't always connect these two memory methods (picturing the meaningful bits—ice cream, jewels, boats—inside, next to, or part of the prominent feature in your mental picture of the person), the effort expended will make the name stick in your mind.

RECALLING NAMES CORRECTLY

Your strategy for remembering a name will be most effective if you continue to rehearse it. Review your appearance notes, images, or name sentences at regular intervals until the name is firmly in mind. When you want to recall the name, it may come to mind automatically or you may need to look carefully at the face and think back to your strategy.

If you memorized appearance notes along with the name, the person's facial features should bring to mind the notes and the name. If you used mental imagery, the face should lead you to remember your initial association between the name and face. If you used the image-name match method, the face should help you recall your image. The prominent feature that you noticed before should be your cue. In your image, that feature will be associated with the meaningful elements in the name. For example, Frances Conner's hair should "look" like ice cream to you and bring to mind her name.

A PITFALL TO AVOID

You can sometimes get into trouble, like my friend who noted the graying sideburns of Mr. Whitehead and called him Mr. Gray the next time she saw him. Similarly, you may picture a crown when meeting Mr. Chown and recall his name as Mr. King.

There are ways to avoid this kind of mistake. You could develop some particular images that you use consistently for common names, such as a blacksmith for Smith and a gardener for Gordon. Your "king" could always wear a purple robe (and then "crown" would never be mistaken for "king"). Another method is to repeat the name in your mind along with your name sentence, so that the latter becomes strongly associated with the correct name. Any time you have a list of people who may be at a meeting, your accuracy, and memory, will be improved by reading over the names in advance.

IF NOTHING WORKS

If the name does not come to mind after examining the face, do not panic. Anxiety interferes tremendously with memory associations. Try to recall the situation in which you first met the person. If you can remember how or where you met him or who introduced you or what you talked about, these associations may jog your memory for the name.

It may help you to go through the alphabet in hopes that one letter will "stick" in your mind more than others. That letter is likely to be the first one in the person's name. Keep it in mind and again focus on prominent facial features as you try to recall your meaningful name sentence or image.

Which Methods Are Best?

I recommend that you start with the simple methods for remembering names, such as paying attention, repeating the name silently, using it in conversation, and writing it down with appearance notes. If you want a greater mental challenge and you want to become skilled at recalling names, practice the more complex strategies until you master them—name sentences, imagery, and the image-name match method.

Once you have perfected a method, work on another one so your techniques can be combined. For example, you could pay attention, repeat the name out loud, and make a name sentence. You could use a name sentence alone if the person doesn't seem to have a remarkable feature and the image-name match method when a feature is obvious. With experience, all the strategies will become quick and easy to use, and you will become the talk of the town!

10

How to Remember
Your Medicine

When my friend Becky's son was about two years old, he developed a painful ear infection. The pediatrician prescribed an antibiotic and emphasized the importance of continuing the medicine three times a day for ten days.

The antibiotic relieved the pain quickly, but once her son seemed well Becky had trouble remembering to give him the medicine. One evening, she realized she had forgotten it completely, so she decided to give the full day's dosage then. "Wouldn't that be just as effective against the germs?" she reasoned. To her horror, it gave the poor child terrible stomach cramps, and both mother and child were awake the entire night.

An experience like Becky's is a reminder of how hard it can be to remember to take (or give) medicine and how important it is to do it

177

at the right time each day. It's no emergency to forget a vitamin pill or to take two. But the medicines prescribed by your doctor may be critical for your health, and failure to take them according to directions may have serious consequences.

Remembering to take medication at particular times each day or on prescribed days is basically a problem of establishing a routine. The routine then becomes your memory aid. Since accidentally taking more than one pill can be as serious as forgetting altogether, you also need to establish a routine to make sure that you take the prescribed dose only once.

REMEMBERING ONE PILL

To establish a pill-taking habit, you have to pay attention to the time. For some people, that is not a problem because their daily schedule requires them to be constantly aware of the clock. All they have to do is take the pill at the same time each day. Other people, especially those who are retired or on vacation, may not want to bother watching the clock.

If you do not normally pay attention to time, you may need to place a clock in an obvious location, set an alarm, attach reminder notes to the refrigerator, or take off your watch and place it on your desk.

Associate Pill with Established Routines

Another solution is to take your medicine in conjunction with activities that are already time-related. It is relatively easy, for example, to remember to take a pill each day at breakfast because you probably eat breakfast at the same table at approximately the same time each day. It makes sense to put your medicine bottle on the kitchen table and take your pill with your orange juice or morning coffee.

Imagery

You can also use imagery as a memory aid. Imagine, for example, the kitchen table with pill bottles dancing on it.

To remember your bedtime pill, establish an image that connects your bed with the medication, such as a life-size pill sleeping in your bed. Whatever image you use needs to be so vivid and so well-practiced that it occurs to you automatically when you see the bed.

Pill Boxes

One easy memory device is a pill container that has seven compartments, each marked with one day of the week. Most drugstores carry them. If the pill is not in the box for a particular day, you will know that you have taken it. It is important to fill the box on the same day each week, *after you've taken that day's pill,* so you'll always know if you've taken the pill for "fill day."

Pill Appointments

If you have a calendar that you refer to every day, put a "P" in the space for each day, and circle the P when you take the pill. An uncircled P tells you that you have not taken the pill yet. For this method to be effective, you should keep the calendar in the same room (or the same purse or pocket) with your pills, and make it a habit to circle the P when you take your medicine.

You will have to work to establish this habit. The first week, place the calendar on the table next to your pills. For the second and third weeks, put the calendar back in its proper place but leave a pencil beside the pills as a reminder. Eventually you will automatically circle the P when you take your pill.

The calendar strategy can also be used with an appointment book. It is particularly helpful if your medicine has to be taken at an odd time, that is, not at mealtimes or bedtime. You can place a large P in your appointment book at each prescribed pill time. If you use your appointment book regularly, you will note the P at the correct time, take your pill, and circle the letter.

The Peg System

For those who are good at creating mental pictures, the peg system (described in Chapter 7) may be a good way to remember whether you have taken your pill. The peg system is a method that matches each number from 1 to 10 with an object. You can create memorable mental pictures that associate those objects with your medication schedule.

Place the bottle where you will see it—by your bed if you take the pill when you get up in the morning or on the kitchen table if you take it at mealtimes.

When you take your pill on September 3rd, imagine the PILL with a TREE because 3 and tree go together in your peg system. If your pill is blue, the tree in your image could be a brilliant blue or BLUE PILLS could be hanging from it like fruit. Be sure that your image shows the pill in some kind of interaction with the tree and is very clear in your mind.

On two-digit dates you'll need to combine peg images. September 15 would combine a bun (1) and hive (5) with the pill. You might imagine a bee HIVE with a queen bee on top; her body is made of a BLUE PILL and she is sitting gloriously on top of her hamburger BUN throne.

Use only one picture at a time, and continue "seeing" that picture as you take your pill. The image should be unique enough so that when you ask yourself the inevitable question an hour later: Did I take my pill today?, you can look at the date, think of the peg(s) for that date, and recall the image easily.

There are four important guidelines for making images that work:
Create the image yourself.
Make the image clear.
Make the image unique or interesting.
Don't create the image until you take your pill.

Don't confuse yourself by mixing up images or by thinking about them and daydreaming about the peg system at other times during the day. The peg system works well because each day's image is distinct, and distinctiveness is an important characteristic of information that is easy to remember.

Images do not duplicate during a month, so it is not likely that you will confuse the images from one month to the next.

The October 1 image has ONE BUN, the October 11 image has TWO BUNS and the October 21 image has A BUN AND A SHOE. Therefore you cannot possibly use the same mental picture again until the next month. When November begins, you will have forgotten the October 1 image, so you can create a new ONE BUN image. This technique also means, of course, that you have to know the date, which isn't a bad thing to note each day.

Verbal Elaboration

To use verbal elaboration for remembering whether you have taken your pill, you need to know the letter-number associations given in Chapter 7 and create a rhyme that connects the pill with the date. Wait until you take the pill to think about your rhyme, and rehearse it repeatedly.

On the first of the month you could say: I TOOK MY PILL, LET'S ROB THE TILL (1=T). As with the peg system, two-digit dates require a combination. For the 18th of the month you would say: I TOOK MY PILL, THE TILL IS FILLED (1=T, 8=F).

REMEMBERING MORE THAN ONE PILL

Pill Boxes

Again, a pill box with seven compartments will come in handy. Fill the box at the beginning of the week. If you take a blue pill twice a day and a white pill four times a day, place one set of all six pills in each compartment. If you take most of your pills with meals you eat at home, leave your pill box on the kitchen table or counter. You will know at the end of each day whether or not you have taken your pills by seeing how many are left in that day's compartment.

If you take your last white pill at bedtime, you could use a second pill box, placing one white pill in each of the seven compartments and keeping the pill box in a prominent place by your bed. (Be sure to leave this pill out of your kitchen pill box.)

Another method is to establish a habit of moving the container (with all six pills in each compartment) to the next place you will take a pill. Therefore, after taking your dinner pills, you will move the pill box to your bed. When you take your bedtime pill, you move it back to the kitchen.

As always, you can establish habits such as these by using persistent reminders around the house until the routine is automatic. Or you can use imagery and picture a huge pill sticking out of your nightstand drawer.

Pill Appointments

A pill container is handy for people who eat most of their meals at home. If you are "out and about" much of the time and are used to keeping an appointment calendar, your best bet is to make pill appointments each day. Your calendar might then read: 12 P.M. BP (blue pill), 4 P.M. WP (white pill). As before, circle the letters when you take each pill. The routine needs to become so automatic that it feels strange to not circle the notation when you take a pill.

You could also write pill appointments on a large calendar if you are at home but do not take pills with meals. Hang the calendar where you see it frequently. Then it will become your cue to ask yourself: HAVE I TAKEN MY PILL?

The Toy Clock Strategy

This is an alternative method for people who are inveterate clock watchers. Go to a school supply store and buy a fairly large toy clock face with movable hands—the kind that is used to teach children how to tell time.

Write your pill schedule on the face of this toy clock (or on a note nearby): 9 A.M. white, 12 P.M. blue, 2 P.M. white, 5 P.M. white.

Set the clock face for 9 A.M. (your first pill) and put it next to the clock you look at most. When the real clock gets close to 9 A.M., check the pill schedule to find out which pill to take, take your pill, and then reset the toy hands to 12 P.M., the time for your next pill.

You will always know whether or not you have taken your pill by looking at the clock face. When it is ahead of the actual time, you're doing just fine, but when it is behind you know that you have forgotten your pill and need to take it right away.

The Peg System

Suppose that you take two red pills and two blue pills each day. You can use the peg system to remember them. The trick with the peg system is to be consistent.

When you take the first blue pill, place a blue pill somewhere in your mental picture. When you take the second blue pill, change the color of some prominent object in your image to blue. Whenever there is no obvious blue object in your image, other than a pill shape, you know that you have not taken your second blue pill.

To see how the system works, imagine this picture for the 8th of the month. As you already know, 8 is a gate. Create each image as you swallow the pill.

First blue pill: picture a child with a BLUE PILL-shaped body, leaning on a GATE in a fence.

First red pill: imagine the RED-PILL-body of another child who has come to play with the BLUE-PILL-child.

Second blue pill: visualize the GATE as BLUE or your two "pill children" painting the GATE BLUE.

Second red pill: imagine that the fence around the GATE is RED.

Let me give you another example. On the 26th of the month, you will build your image around a SHOE and STICKS (2 is a shoe, 6 is sticks).

First blue pill: imagine a large BLUE PILL filling up the inside of a laced-up SHOE that is sitting on a pile of STICKS.

First red pill: imagine it as the RED tongue of the SHOE.

Second blue pill: visualize the SHOE (or the laces) in a bright BLUE color.

Second red pill: imagine that the STICKS are RED. Or picture the STICKS below the SHOE going up in smoke, with RED flames all around the BLUE SHOE with the RED tongue and the BLUE PILL inside the shoe. You won't forget a picture like that one!

As you can see, this memory strategy requires complex images, but it's well worth it. Practicing the technique can make it easier for you to create images, and it will give your mind a challenge.

When not to use the peg system. The peg system won't be effective if you have a large number of pills to take or more than two different colors are involved. Although you could add more and more pill shapes here and there, it becomes too complicated to create a memorable image with a large number of similar items.

Drawing Pictures

If you like to draw, you may be able to compose a picture that includes the pills you have taken and the peg pictures (bun, shoe, tree, etc.). You could have fun adding an unlimited number of pills to the picture. You wouldn't need to recall the picture because you could keep it in a prominent place and add more to the picture as you take your pills.

Another creative way to remember pills is to draw a picture that incorporates the pills with the date. For example, on the first of the month, a dancing number "1" could be kicking pills in the air. On the 8th of the month, an "8" could be drawn around pills on an ice rink.

Method of Loci

If you like the idea of using mental imagery but have five or more pills to remember each day or three or more of the same color, you could use the method of loci. Although this technique is normally used for recalling a list, it can be very useful if you have no trouble remembering to take a pill on time but forget whether or not you have already taken it.

First select a series of familiar locations that you can "walk through" mentally. As I walk clockwise around my living room, for example, I come to the rocking chair and love seat, then the piano, stereo, book case, and, finally, the sofa and hutch. If I were trying to remember a list of seven pills, I would use mental imagery to associate each of these room locations, in turn, with one pill (there must be as many locations as there are pills).

First pill, taken at 9 A.M.: imagine a BLUE PILL in the ROCKING CHAIR

Second pill, taken at 12 P.M.: match it with the LOVE SEAT (and so on around the room)

That sounds easy enough, but the trouble with simply matching the pill to the location is that it is difficult to tell one day's image from the next. The images you used the first day would be appropriate for the second and third day as well. Pretty soon you would have no idea if you were remembering the pill you took today or yesterday.

Combine pegs and loci. To prevent this confusion, you can combine pegs and loci. On the fourth of the month, these might be your images (remember, 4 is DOOR):

First (blue) pill: imagine a large BLUE DOOR under the ROCKING CHAIR.

Second (white) pill: imagine trying to push the LOVE SEAT through a tiny WHITE DOORWAY.

As you take each pill on the fourth, you create images that match each location with a door. Again, the more unique your image, the more likely you are to remember it.

When you're not sure whether you took your last pill, number 5 for the day, think about the fifth location, the bookcase. If the image that most readily comes to mind is a tree standing on top of a bookcase (on the 3rd of the month all your images included a tree), you have not taken that pill on the fourth.

On the 17th of the month, you could imagine a BUN and an ANGEL in each location as you take the corresponding pill (1 is a bun, 7 is heaven). When you take the fourth pill (the fourth loci is the stereo), you might imagine, for example, an ANGEL sitting on top of a RECORD as it goes around on a BUN turntable. If thinking of the stereo does not get you an image of an ANGEL and a BUN, or if you get the 1 + 6 image, you will know that you have not taken the fourth pill on the 17th.

To use this method effectively, you must use the same locations every time. The first pill must *always* be the rocking chair and the third must *always* be the piano. Wait until you take your pill, and then and only then develop your image. When you practice the technique, use a different set of locations or use the same loci associated with different items.

You should also avoid daydreaming about all the possible mental pictures you could use connecting your loci with peg system pictures. This might be fun, but it spoils the unique association between taking your pill and creating a particular image.

Using loci in your house provides an added advantage: any time you walk into that room you will ask yourself, Have I taken my pill?

Combine Methods

You need not feel that any one of these pill-taking mnemonics should be used to the exclusion of others. It may be that you are normally at home and remember your pills easily because your seven-container pill box sits on the kitchen table. When you go out, however, you may need extra help from mental imagery or the method of loci.

To remember to take your 12 P.M. pill when you are having lunch with a friend on the 10th, just imagine your friend riding on a HEN that has a big PILL in its mouth (10 is a hen in the peg system). When you see your friend, your odd picture should come to mind almost automatically and remind you to take your pill.

Make Your Methods A Habit

I have described both simple and elaborate methods for remembering to take pills and for remembering that you have taken them. A simple method may be sufficient. But if none of them works for you, you will need to apply more effort. Try some of the complex techniques, such as associating pills with locations in your house.

Whatever strategy you choose will only be effective if you use it regularly. You have to make it a habit to take your pills with particular meals or to check your calendar or to create visual images. Habits can only be established through consistent practice.

11

Maintaining Your Memory Power

I hope that by now you've tried some of the memory techniques described in this book and been successful with them. Merely reading the book, without practicing, will teach you about memory, but it's doubtful that your ability to remember will change, just as reading an exercise book won't get your body in shape.

Neither will a one-day memory course permanently improve skills. It's like a crash diet. Just as you gain back the weight because you haven't changed your eating habits, so you fall back on your old techniques even though they may not be very powerful for remembering. Only with deliberate effort and regular practice will you integrate newly learned techniques into your usual memory activities. The way to change your memory power permanently is to make strategy usage a routine part of your everyday life.

When you become skilled at using mnemonics, they will become a natural part of your daily interaction with your world. You won't have to devote any conscious mental energy to figuring out how to apply a strategy. You'll be able to use strategies automatically, just as you drive a car without thinking about each minute detail. Images will come to mind spontaneously, peg words will associate easily with items to be learned, numbers will translate quickly into letters and words.

When you can apply strategies effortlessly, the effect of aging is minimized. The slower thinking associated with aging has little impact on skills you're able to use automatically. In addition, well-learned strategies are not likely to be forgotten as you get older.

HOW TO PRACTICE

You should approach learning to use memory strategies as you would any new skill—learn one step at a time and practice often and regularly.

Start simple. Select one strategy that you already know but do not use as often or as effectively as you should. Use it for several fairly simple memory tasks, such as three errands, two names, delivering a message, or relating a news item. You may not *need* the strategy as a memory aid, but use it anyway, for practice.

During your practice period, don't risk failure by depending upon this strategy. For anything important, use a back-up strategy you can depend on (perhaps writing a note).

Continue applying this strategy to simple tasks until you develop some self-confidence. Then try it out on harder tasks, such as learning to operate your new computer or studying for a licensing exam. When you find yourself comfortable with this strategy, continue practicing until you can apply it very quickly.

Use this same procedure for a second strategy. A third. A fourth. After you're good at using several of them, you can use the following procedures to compare how effective they are for you.

Use different methods for learning the same material. Select a magazine story, newspaper editorial, or anything else that consists of at least five paragraphs, each covering different information. (You could also use this approach to learn a list of names, for example, applying different methods to learn two or three names each day.)

On day 1, outline paragraph one and see how much you remember two hours later.

On day 2, use the PQRST method on the second paragraph and test yourself two hours later.

On day 3, try mental imagery for the third paragraph, and so on.

Always test yourself so that you can identify the method that leads to highest recall as well as the most rapid learning.

Use one strategy all day. Each day use a different strategy to remember everything: errands, groceries, medicines, appointments, routes, newspaper articles. Use it for both learning and recall. Try the peg system on Monday, verbal elaboration on Tuesday, your memory place on Wednesday. At the end of the day, note your successes and failures.

How to Remember to Practice

You have already read about using internal or external cues to remember information or errands. Now apply the same principles to remembering to practice the strategies that you normally don't think of using. The following examples will give you an idea of how to remind yourself to use several strategies. You should be able to think of ways to cue yourself for others.

Imagery. Until you regularly think of using imagery as a memory device, put this book on top of the TV set to remind you to practice creating mental pictures of events on the screen. Associate the "eye" of the TV screen with making images in your "mind's eye." Let the face on your clock, your face in the mirror, or faces in photographs cue you to use imagery for faces.

Verbal elaboration. Remind yourself to use verbal elaboration by taking your dictionary off the bookshelf and putting it in some unusual but highly visible place. Or write a list of ten words for which you want to learn the definitions, and tape the list to your phone as a reminder. You should actually learn the definitions, thereby practicing verbal elaboration and, as an added benefit, improving your vocabulary. Soon you'll find yourself spontaneously using verbal elaboration in a variety of situations.

Calendar habit. To remind yourself to use a calendar, post a very large calendar with striking pictures where you can't help noticing it. Draw three small circles on each day for an entire month. Check it at least three times each day, crossing off one circle each time. Circles that are blank at the end of the day will indicate how many times you forgot.

For practice, use the calendar for recording birthdays, regular weekly meetings, and other events that you are likely to remember anyway, even if you recall that information internally. Use it for errands and the names of people you meet. The more you write there, the sooner you will begin to use it habitually. Once your habit is established, you can get a smaller calendar or move it to a less prominent place.

Memory place. Put a large box or basket in a location where it will be obvious. In the beginning, keep a note pad in it and write down the date each time you look there. Keep items in the basket that you need every day (reading glasses, watch, keys) so you get in the habit of using it daily. Make an image of these items interacting with the basket. Every time you find the objects there without searching for them, the value of the basket is reinforced.

MAKING MEMORY DECISIONS

Memory success depends on more than knowing how to use strategies effectively. It also depends on knowing when to apply them, and selecting the most suitable method for the situation. Ask yourself: Do I want to remember this? What strategy should I select? How can I minimize forgetting?

Do I Want to Remember This?

If you never ask yourself this question, you are not paying attention to how you use your memory, and that will prevent you from making the most of your memory power. You can't answer yes all the time without overloading your memory. But if your answer is always no, you will eventually lose memory power due to insufficient "exercise."

Your memory needs a regular workout. If you find you are not using your memory very much, make a conscious effort to remember five to eight things each day. At least every other day include these three types of memory tasks: recall an event from your past, learn some new information, remember to carry out an activity that is not routine. Your goal is to obtain memory stimulation without overloading to the point of failure.

To some extent, motivation can direct your choice of what to remember:

You learn new procedures at work to increase your efficiency; you memorize your part in a play so you won't forget your lines; you concentrate on "Computer Chronicles" on TV because you enjoy being a hacker in your spare time; you remember every detail when you meet Beverly Sills because you want to share the experience with your niece, who has idolized her for years.

Your own memory skills may also guide your decision about what to remember. Don't set yourself up for failure.

If you have trouble remembering what you hear, you don't offer to tell a friend all about a lecture; if you can never remember patterns or pictures, don't shop for curtains for a friend.

What Strategy Should I Select?

Once you have decided to remember something, carefully consider ways to accomplish your goal. Your strategy should be one that works well for you and suits the kind—and importance—of the material you want to remember. Don't overload your memory by using a more complex strategy than the situation calls for.

Simple tasks call for simple strategies. There is no need to overburden your mind with internal strategies for the following:

Drop off clothes at cleaners: Put the clothes in the car while you are thinking of it. Seeing them will remind you.

Weekly shopping at supermarket: Keep a list. When you make the decision to shop, put the list where it will be noticed, in your purse or in your memory place.

Dentist appointment: Mark it on your calendar and carry the calendar with you. Or write on cardboard in big red letters, DENTIST 10:30, and keep the sign in easy sight.

Intermediate strategies can be used for small memory tasks. They may be internal or combine internal and external methods.

Name of your spouse's new secretary: Use an internal strategy such as verbal elaboration or association, but write the name down as a backup.

Route from vacation house to nearest town (route is poorly marked and there are few places to drive off the road to consult a map): Before leaving the house memorize the route, using visualization. Bring the map in case you get lost.

Sometimes you need complex strategies, or combinations of strategies.

Meeting new in-laws at the engagement party: Make sure you have a list. Memorize appearance notes with help from your son or daughter.

Awards acceptance speech (to look unrehearsed you can't use notes): Use the method of loci, peg system, or verbal elaboration to remember elements of your talk in order.

Routines to teach aerobic dance class: Use visualization to remember the dance steps and use the peg system to recall the order.

Names of people and their accomplishments for test in history course: Make rhyming mnemonics to match them.

Use external strategies whenever they will aid recall. Use internal strategies when information needs to be remembered for a long time and/or has to be recalled in situations where external cues or notes cannot be used (such as a test).

HOW CAN I MINIMIZE FORGETTING?

The answer is to rehearse your strategy and test yourself at regular intervals. Make changes in the mnemonic if it doesn't seem memorable enough to you or if you think of a better technique.

When you rehearse, review the original information you learned: I need to go by the bank, pick up tickets at Piedmont Airlines, and call the kennel, as well as the mnemonic you selected. Using first letter associations, your mnemonic was PHI BETA KAPPA (PBK).

Start with a short interval between rehearsal sessions. Gradually increase it until it is the same length of time as you will have between your last review and the time of recall.

Make the practice test context as similar as you can to the recall context you are expecting. If you are giving a speech before a large audience, ask your family members to be your audience.

Creating a more powerful memory will be easier if you have the cooperation and assistance of friends and family. Explain to them what you are doing, and enlist their help. You want them to know why there are suddenly notes on the back door, old photographs on the TV set, and a calendar on the kitchen table. Once they see your energetic determination they may want to improve their own memories too!

Utilize your potential for lifelong memory strength. Vigilant self-awareness and persistent efforts to provide memory stimulation can prevent serious memory loss for most people.

To maintain your memory power at any age, stay aware, keep your mind and memory stimulated, keep your attention skills at their peak, and use memory strategies regularly. That is the only way to maintain your memory power. There's no magic pill, and no simple gimmick. But with a bit of effort, memory success can be habit-forming.

Glossary

Acquisition—See Learning.

Age changes—Increases or decreases in test scores that occur as a person gets older.

Age differences—Performance variations between young and old research participants.

Alzheimer's disease—A condition that leads to progressive mental deterioration as a result of brain cell malfunctions and chemical changes. Also called senile dementia of the Alzheimer's type (SDAT).

Amnesia—A disability (usually the result of a head injury or trauma) in which an individual may forget specific events from the past and/or be unable to learn new information.

Association—Connecting new information to something already known. It is through association (to a present experience) that old memories suddenly pop into your mind.

Automatic pilot—Doing routine activities without being alert and without paying attention to one's surroundings or actions.

Chunking—A type of organization in which letters, digits, or words are grouped into units that are easy to remember.

Combined rehearsal—A memory strategy for lists. As each new item is added to the list, it is repeated along with earlier list items.

Cue—A word, picture, smell, song, or anything related to or associated with information or events to be remembered. When a cue is available, it aids recall.

Cued recall—Type of recall test in which hints or clues are provided to aid retrieval.

Dementia—Mental deterioration characterized by memory problems, disorientation, and/or disturbances of mood and personality.

Distributed practice—Several rehearsal sessions spread over a long period.

Encoding—See Learning.

Episodic memory—Recall of particular events or information learned at a specific time and place.

External strategy—Any memory strategy that relies on information stored outside of your head. The primary external strategies are writing, organizing the environment, and using object cues.

Free recall—Type of memory test in which there are no cues to support retrieval. A person simply remembers everything that he can.

Gerontologist—Specialist in the study of aging.

Idiot savant—A person who is mentally retarded but who has mastered some single, particular kind of intellectual or artistic skill.

Image-name match method—Memory strategy for names that involves creating an image of a person's face (focusing on a prominent feature), finding meaningful words embedded in the name, and forming a new, expanded image that links the prominent feature with the meaningful words.

Immediate memory—A memory storage system that has a limited capacity of five to nine items. Information is retained in immediate memory for as long as attention is paid to it and for up to one minute after attention is shifted.

Incidental learning—Remembering that occurs without any intention or effort to memorize.

Interactive imagery—A memory strategy in which one mental picture combines related to-be-remembered items.

Interference—Difficulty in recalling particular information because it is similar to other material that has been learned.

Internal speech—Talking to oneself while doing a complex task as a way of keeping track of what needs to be done.

Intentional learning—Deliberate memorization.

Internal strategy—Any memory strategy in which information is retained inside your head. The primary internal strategies are association, organization, mental imagery, verbal elaboration, and rote repetition.

Learning—Getting information into your mind for the first time. Also called encoding or acquisition.

Long-term memory—A memory storage system that has an unlimited capacity to retain information for extended time periods.

Memory place—A location or container specifically designated for keeping items you want to find at a later time.

Memory power—Ability to memorize new material, to retain information for long time periods, and to recall items at will.

Memory repertoire—Set of strategies that are used by an individual for most of his everyday memory tasks.

Mental imagery—Visualization, or getting a picture into your mind.

Method of loci—Memory strategy that involves associating new information to familiar locations through mental imagery.

Mnemonic—Any specific technique that improves memory.

Mnemonist—A memory expert who systematically and efficiently applies strategies to remember considerably more than the average person.

Multi-infarct dementia—Mental deterioration caused by multiple strokes.

Name sentence—Memory strategy in which a person's name is translated, through verbal elaboration, into meaningful words that are then used in a sentence.

Object cue—Any item used to aid recall of information, such as a shoe (to remind you to jog), a timer, or a photograph album.

Organization—The combination of several pieces of information into groups of items that are logically related.

Overlearning—Studying information repeatedly even after it has been committed to memory.

Overload—The condition of having too many memory tasks to do at the same time.

Peg system—A memory strategy that involves matching numbers with objects, and associating to-be-remembered items to those objects through mental imagery.

Photographic memory—The ability to hold an exact image of an entire page in your mind.

PQRST method—Memory strategy used for reading material. The letters stand for Preview, Question, Read, State, and Test.

Prospective memory—Remembering to complete a task that has been planned for a later time.

Rate of forgetting—The speed at which learned information is forgotten.

Recall—The memory stage in which you try to bring back to mind information that has been learned.

Recognition—Type of recall test in which learned (old) items have to be identified in a set of old and new items.

Reconstruction—A process that occurs during recall, in which new associations and cues that are part of the recall context are added to your memory for the recalled information.

Rehearsal—Reviewing the strategy applied and the specific mnemonic generated during initial learning.

Remembering—Lay term used to refer to learning, retention, and/or recall.

Retention—Storage of what has been learned.

Retrieval—See Recall.

Rote repetition—Memory strategy of repeating information exactly as it was given.

Savings—Information retained in long-term memory from initial learning, which makes relearning faster.

Search—Looking through your mind for information that has been learned.

Search efficiency—The degree to which a person searches longer for information when he is sure that he has learned it or has some previous knowledge about it.

Selective testing—Type of self-testing in which you test on all the information learned, then test only on the parts not recalled easily on previous tests.

Self-paced—Experimental condition in which the research participant controls the amount of time available for learning or recall.

Semantic memory—Retrieval of words, concepts, and categories, learned gradually through everyday experience.

Senile dementia of the Alzheimer's type (SDAT)—See Alzheimer's disease.

Senile dementia—Dementia that is diagnosed in an older person.

Senility—The lay term for senile dementia.

Short-term memory—See Immediate memory.

Strategy—Any method or technique that enhances learning, retention, or recall.

Subject—A person who participates in experimental research.

Verbal elaboration—Memory strategy in which meaningful verbal information is added to items that need to be learned, thus creating a memorable word, sentence, story, or poem.

Verbalizer—A person who remembers best by using words, letters, and stories to link items that he wants to learn.

Visualizer—A person who memorizes best by using mental pictures.

World knowledge—Any information that is learned through life experiences, for example, language, movie trivia, or historical facts.

Reference Notes

Chapter 1

If you are interested in learning more about the way memory works, there are several academic (Gruneberg, Morris, & Sykes, 1978; Kail, 1979; Zechmeister & Nyberg, 1982) and lay books on the subject (Higbee, 1977; Loftus, 1980; Neisser, 1982). As a case study, Luria's book on the mnemonist, *S,* is fascinating (Luria, 1968).

My characterization of memory is based on an information processing viewpoint (Lachman, Lachman, & Butterfield, 1979), combined with elements of the constructive (Bransford, 1979) and levels-of-processing approaches (Cermak & Craik, 1979).

Many of the experiments presented here, and in the following chapters, represent typical methods used to investigate memory, and are not descriptions of particular studies. I will cite the specific research, where appropriate, or give you the author's name if several similar studies have been conducted by the same investigator. You can then find his/her citations in the references below.

In this chapter, the only specific experiment I presented demonstrates how *reconstructive memory affects eyewitness testimony,* based on the research of Loftus (e.g., Loftus & Palmer, 1974).

Chapter 2

There are many complex issues involved in the selection of a research design for examining age changes over the lifespan. These issues are thoroughly discussed in textbooks on aging (e.g., Hultsch & Deutsch, 1981). My description of the usual research practices of gerontologists is based on surveys of the psychological literature (Abrahams, Hoyer, Elias, & Bradigan, 1975; Hoyer, Raskind, & Abrahams, 1984).

Comparable performance by volunteers and nonvolunteers was obtained in a study investigating a variety of intelligence and memory measures (Lachman, Lachman, & Taylor, 1982).

To find out more about the correspondence between intelligence and memory research, see Botwinick (1984) and Salthouse (1982).

Individual factors that affect memory test performance have been examined in light of a new emphasis on plasticity or performance variability (Willis & Baltes, 1980). Practice, by itself, can improve memory performance (e.g., Camp, Markley, & Kramer, 1983; Treat, Poon, Fozard, & Popkin, 1978), and a person with higher education and a large vocabulary will perform better than his less knowledgable age cohorts (Bowles & Poon, 1982; Gonda, Quayhagen, & Schaie, 1981; Poon & Fozard, 1980). As described in this chapter, older adults can perform better when *test materials are made more meaningful by allowing participants to select their own items to learn* (Perlmuter, 1985), and by using *words that are matched to the older adults' vocabulary* (Barrett & Wright, 1981). Gerontologists are becoming increasingly aware of motivational differences between young and old on unfamiliar laboratory tasks (cf. Hultsch & Pentz, 1980; Schaie, 1978). Concern about the artificiality of laboratory conditions has led to more exploration of the relationship between experimental findings and everyday memory (Gruneberg & Morris, 1979; Gruneberg, Morris, & Sykes, 1978; Harris & Morris, 1984; Hulicka, 1982; Kausler, in press). The studies that examined *spatial memory in familiar and unfamiliar environments* were done by Kirasic (Kirasic & Allen, in press). *My everyday memory findings are based on in-home interviews* (West, 1984; West & Walton, 1985).

Chapter 3

The best source for reviews of all aspects of memory is *New Directions in Memory and Aging* (Poon, Fozard, Cermak, Arenberg, & Thompson, 1980).

You can read more about the effects of reduced speed in *Aging in the 1980s* (Poon, 1980a). One good example of slowing is the experiment I described in which *older adults required 23 practice periods to learn as compared to 8 needed by younger adults under rapid recall conditions* (Monge & Hultsch, 1971). The chess study I presented is based on research by Charness (Charness, 1981a, b). The value of practice and task familiarity in the workplace is demonstrated in several studies by Murrell (e.g., Murrell, 1970). The importance of familiarity is also indicated by evidence that older adults scan letters arranged alphabetically much faster than they scan letters arranged randomly (Thomas, Waugh, & Fozard, 1978). Perlmuter (1985) has demonstrated the effects of increased motivation on learning speed.

There is considerable debate at the moment about whether or not speed is the central factor in age-related cognitive change. Salthouse, among others, argues that losses in speed account for reduced use of strategies, and encoding and retrieval deficits (Salthouse, 1980). Arenberg, among others, argues that losses in speed are the *result* rather than the cause of changes in strategy usage (Arenberg, 1980).

Under the topic of strategy changes, I describe research in which older and younger adults *learn a list by using questions that are related to the meaning of the words on the list* (West & Boatwright, 1983). There are also numerous studies on this topic by Craik (see Craik & Simon, 1980). Simon (1979) conducted the experiment in which young adults were unable to use strategies when *presentation time was cut to four seconds*. For confirmation of the disuse hypothesis, see the work of Langer and Avorn and others (e.g., Avorn, 1982; Murrell & Humphries, 1978; Treat, Poon, Fozard, & Popkin, 1978). The benefits of memory training have been discussed in many articles by Poon (Poon, 1980b; Poon, Walsh-Sweeney, & Fozard, 1980; Treat, Poon, Fozard, & Popkin, 1978).

Numerous reviews are available for the attention research, if you would like to learn more (Craik, 1977; Hoyer & Plude, 1980; Kinsbourne, 1980). Arenberg (1980) discusses aging and attention, distractibility, and interference.

The verbal learning literature clearly shows slower acquisition by older adults (see Kausler, 1982). Also, *discrimination learning studies using letter stimuli, such as the one described with the O and X,* demonstrate that older adults take longer to learn than younger adults. Strategies appear to be the reason. For example, older adults are less likely to use sophisticated hypothesis testing strategies on discrimination learning problems (Gholson, 1980).

The best articles on the importance of retrieval support and cues can be found in *Aging and Cognitive Processes* (Craik & Byrd, 1982; Perlmutter & Mitchell, 1982). Both experiments demonstrating the *importance of cues for older adults* were done in my laboratory (West & Boatwright, 1983; West & Cohen, 1985). The investigation of *easy and hard recognition and recall* was reported at the 1984 meeting of the APA (Craik, 1984).

It is clear that aging is not associated with increased forgetting of information stored in immediate memory (Kausler, 1982). The *lack of immediate memory deficits (based on recall of the last few words in a list)* is explained by Craik (1977).

Forgetting rates have been examined using a number of different approaches: *varying the time intervals between study and test* (Hulicka & Weiss, 1965), measuring *savings* (Caird, 1966), and *varying the number of intervening items between repeated presentations of the same word in a list* (Poon & Fozard,

1980). My conclusion—forgetting of well-learned information does not vary with age—is consistent with that of Kausler (1982, pp. 396–399).

There is an excellent review of the early investigations of world knowledge (called remote memory) by Erber (1981). Intelligence tests that measure world knowledge are called tests of crystallized abilities, and such tests show little, if any, age decline (Horn & Cattell, 1967).

The evidence for serial and exhaustive search is based on the Sternberg paradigm, in which response reaction times (after studying item sets of different sizes) indicate the number of items that are mentally reviewed during a memory search. Sternberg's original research was conducted with student subjects (Sternberg, 1970), but *older adults' short-term memory searches are also serial and exhaustive* (Anders, Fozard, & Lillyquist, 1972). The search efficiency research I described is based on the Lachmans' work (e.g., Lachman & Lachman, 1980).

The section on interference explains a study in which *recall of a list is tested after six or two successive lists* are presented, and another study in which *several intervening tasks have to be performed between learning and recall.* To see examples of this kind, read Hulicka (1967) and Mistler-Lachman (1977).

Chapter 4

Bandura has systematically investigated the effects of self-concept—self-efficacy—on performance (e.g., Bandura, 1982). This chapter is based on his work and recent articles on self-efficacy among the aged (Berry, West, & Scogin, 1983; Lachman & Jelalian, 1984; Rebok & Offerman, 1983). The general relationship between self-report and performance has been examined from a number of points of view (cf. Chaffin & Herrmann, 1983; Dixon & Hultsch, 1983a, b; Perlmutter, 1978; West, Boatwright, & Schleser, 1984; Zarit, Cole, & Guider, 1981; Zelinski, Gilewski, & Thompson, 1980), and there is concern that negative memory self-evaluations may be quite common among the elderly (Cavanaugh, Grady, & Perlmutter, 1983; Hulicka, 1982; Perlmutter, 1980).

Your environment can have a significant impact on your memory ability by providing cues, appropriate memory tasks, and social support (Fozard & Thomas, 1975; Lawton & Nahemow, 1973). The importance of maintaining mental stimulation in one's environment is emphasized by the recent research of Langer and Avorn (e.g., Avorn, 1982). Institutional care can result in an environment lacking in memory challenge (Langer & Avorn, 1982; Winocur, 1982).

Chapter 5

The best book on living with Alzheimer's (for the general public) is *The 36 Hour Day* (Mace & Robins, 1981), which recommends a whole host of methods for families of the SDAT patient. Many academic books explain the difficulties inherent in differential diagnosis of Alzheimer's and the effects of drugs, depression, and physical disorders on memory (Birren &

Schaie, 1985; Miller & Cohen, 1981; Poon, 1980a; Storandt, Siegler, & Elias, 1978).

The investigation of the *effects of cardiovascular problems on the ability of pilots* is an old study (Spieth, 1965) whereas *efforts to improve cognitive performance by improving cardiovascular functioning* have begun relatively recently (Dustman et al., 1984).

Perceptual deficits are described well in textbooks (e.g., Huyck & Hoyer, 1982). The influence of emotional state on memory has been discussed in a number of papers, some of which specifically show that memory will improve when anxiety and depression are reduced (Popkin, Gallagher, Thompson, & Moore, 1982; Yesavage, Rose, & Spiegel, 1982).

Chapter 6

The distinction between internal and external strategies is quite common (e.g., Harris, 1984; Morris, 1979). Self-report questionnaires, interviews, diaries, and experiments have indicated the strategies that most people typically use (Cavanaugh, Grady, & Perlmutter, 1983; Harris, 1980; West, 1984). While there is some doubt about the value of self-report questionnaires as an accurate indicator of performance (Morris, 1984), my own experience in training groups suggests that diaries and practice exercises can be a beneficial way to find out more about your abilities. There is also some evidence that diaries are more accurate than questionnaires or interviews and that daily record-keeping improves self-awareness (Carp & Carp, 1981).

The standards for performance indicated for the tests are based on interviews I conducted with these tests and similar tasks (West & Walton, 1985).

Chapter 7

Although some of the strategies described in this chapter are new, most of them are commonly accepted and every method has been used as a memory aid by at least some of the older adults participating in my memory training classes. For some of the techniques, there is specific research demonstrating that older and/or middle-aged people can benefit from practicing the strategies. Evidence of this kind is available for interactive imagery (see Poon, Walsh-Sweeney, & Fozard, 1980; Yesavage, 1985), object cues and notes (Moscovitch, 1982; West, 1984), organization (Hultsch, 1969; Schmitt, Murphy, & Sanders, 1981), verbal elaboration (Canestrari, 1968; Hellebusch, 1976; Hulicka & Grossman, 1967), the peg system (Hellebusch, 1976), and the method of loci (Anschutz, Camp, Markley, & Kramer, in press; Robertson-Tchabo, Hausman, & Arenberg, 1976; Smith, Heckhausen, Kliegl, & Baltes, 1984). These strategies have also been used to improve the everyday abilities of memory impaired individuals (Wilson & Moffat, 1984).

Most memory improvement books for the general public have focused exclusively on internal strategies for learning (cf. Cermak, 1976; Higbee,

1977; Lorayne & Lucas, 1974), although external aids are clearly very useful (Harris, 1978, 1984). Distributed practice has been known to be effective for some time (see Zechmeister & Nyberg, 1982). My argument for the importance of reinstating learning conditions is based on several established principles: encoding specificity (Tulving & Thompson, 1973), transfer appropriate processing (Morris, Bransford, & Franks, 1977) and state dependent recall (Bower, 1981). Investigations with adults indicate that feeling-of-knowing states are usually accurate (Lachman & Lachman, 1980). Also, memory diaries have suggested that the most effective way to get around tip-of-the-tongue blocking states is to use alternative associations (Reason & Lucas, 1984). Reason (1984) discusses the memory value of routines.

Chapter 8

The most extensive work on absent-mindedness can be found in Reason's writings (e.g., Reason, 1984). Factors related to attention training are described in the Wilson and Moffat book (1984). My recommendation to use task-directed internal speech is based on self-instructional training methods (Meichenbaum, 1974).

Chapter 9

Variations on imagery techniques have been used in most of the studies training older adults to remember names (for a review, see Yesavage, 1985).

Chapter 10

My recommendations for remembering pills are a natural extension of the techniques described in Chapter 7, and are not based on any studies designed to improve memory for medicines.

Chapter 11

Although their book is addressed to psychologists and health professionals working with head injury patients, Wilson and Moffat (1984) offer some other suggestions for ways to identify your strengths and establish a program for memory improvement.

Bibliography

Abrahams, J. P., Hoyer, W. J., Elias, M. F., & Bradigan, B. (1975). Gerontological research in psychology published in the Journal of Gerontology 1963–74: Perspectives and progress. *Journal of Gerontology, 30,* 668–673.

Anders, T. R., Fozard, J. L., & Lillyquist, T. D. (1972). Effects of age upon retrieval from short-term memory. *Developmental Psychology, 6,* 214–217.

Anschutz, L., Camp, C. J., Markley, R. P., & Kramer, J. J. (in press). Maintenance and generalization of mnemonics for grocery shopping by older adults. *Experimental Aging Research.*

Arenberg, D. (1980). Comments on the processes that account for memory declines with age. In L. W. Poon, J. L. Fozard, L. S. Cermak, D. Arenberg, & L. W. Thompson (Eds.), *New directions in memory and aging: Proceedings of the George A. Talland Memorial Conference.* Hillsdale, NJ: Lawrence Erlbaum Assoc.

Avorn, J. (1982). Studying cognitive performance in the elderly: A biopsychosocial approach. In F. I. M. Craik & S. Trehub (Eds.), *Aging and cognitive processes.* New York: Plenum Press.

Bahrick, H. P. (1984). Memory for people. In J. E. Harris & P. E. Morris

(Eds.), *Everyday memory, actions and absent-mindedness.* London: Academic Press.

Bandura, A. (1981). Self-referent thought: A developmental analysis of self-efficacy. In J. H. Flavell & L. Ross (Eds.), *Social cognitive development: Frontiers and possible futures.* Cambridge, England: Cambridge University Press.

Bandura, A. (1982). Self-efficacy mechanism in human agency. *American Psychologist, 37,* 122–147.

Bandura, A., Reese, L., & Adams, N. E. (1982). Microanalysis of action and fear arousal as a function of differential levels of perceived self-efficacy. *Journal of Personality and Social Psychology, 43,* 5–21.

Barrett, T. R., & Wright, M. (1981). Age-related facilitation in recall following semantic processing. *Journal of Gerontology, 36,* 194–199.

Berry, J., West, R., & Scogin, F. (1983, November). Predicting everyday and laboratory memory skill. Paper presented at the meeting of the Gerontological Society of America, San Francisco.

Birren, J. E., & Schaie, K. W. (1985). *Handbook of the psychology of aging* (2nd ed.). New York: Van Nostrand Reinhold.

Botwinick, J. (1984). *Aging and behavior* (3rd ed.). New York: Springer.

Bower, G. H. (1981). Mood and memory. *American Psychologist, 36,* 129–148.

Bowles, N. L., & Poon, L. W. (1982). An analysis of the effect of aging on recognition memory. *Journal of Gerontology, 37,* 212–219.

Bransford, J. D. (1979). *Human cognition.* Belmont, CA: Wadsworth.

Caird, W. K. (1966). Aging and short-term memory. *Journal of Gerontology, 21,* 295–299.

Camp, C. J., Markley, R. P., & Kramer, J. J. (1983). Spontaneous use of mnemonics by elderly individuals. *Educational Gerontology, 9,* 57–71.

Canestrari, R. E., Jr. (1968). Age changes in acquisition. In G. A. Talland (Ed.), *Human aging and behavior.* New York: Academic Press.

Carp, F. M., & Carp, A. (1981). The validity, reliability and generalizability of diary data. *Experimental Aging Research, 7,* 281–287.

Cavanaugh, J. C., Grady, J. G., & Perlmutter, M. (1983). Forgetting and use of memory aids in 20- to 70-year olds' everyday life. *International Journal of Aging and Human Development, 17,* 113–122.

Cermak, L. S. (1976). *Improving your memory.* New York: McGraw-Hill.

Cermak, L. S., & Craik, F. I. M. (1979). *Levels of processing in human memory.* Hillsdale, NJ: Lawrence Erlbaum Assoc.

Chaffin, R., & Herrmann, D. J. (1983). Self reports of memory abilities by old and young adults. *Human Learning, 2,* 17–28.

Charness, N. (1981a). Aging and skilled problem solving. *Journal of Experimental Psychology: General, 110,* 21–38.

Charness, N. (1981b). Visual short-term memory and aging in chess players. *Journal of Gerontology, 36,* 615–619.

Craik, F. I. M. (1977). Age differences in human memory. In J. E. Birren & K. W. Schaie (Eds.), *Handbook of the psychology of aging.* New York: Van Nostrand Reinhold.

Craik, F. I. M. (1984, August). Aging and memory: An interactive approach. Paper presented at the meetings of the American Psychological Association, Toronto.

Craik, F. I. M., & Byrd, M. (1982). Aging and cognitive deficits: The role of attentional resources. In F. I. M. Craik & S. Trehub (Eds.), *Aging and cognitive processes.* New York: Plenum Press.

Craik, F. I. M., & Simon, E. (1980). Age differences in memory: The roles of attention and depth of processing. In L. W. Poon, J. L. Fozard, L. S. Cermak, D. Arenberg, & L. W. Thompson (Eds.), *New directions in memory and aging: Proceedings of the George A. Talland Memorial Conference.* Hillsdale, NJ: Lawrence Erlbaum Assoc.

Craik, F. I. M., & Trehub, S. (Eds.) (1982). *Aging and cognitive processes.* New York: Plenum Press.

Dixon, R. A., & Hultsch, D. F. (1983a). Structure and development of metamemory in adulthood. *Journal of Gerontology, 38,* 682–688.

Dixon, R. A., & Hultsch, D. F. (1983b). Metamemory and memory for text relationships in adulthood: A cross-validation study. *Journal of Gerontology, 38,* 689–694.

Dustman, R. E., Ruhling, R. O., Russell, E. M., Shearer, D. E., Bonekat, H. W., Shigeoka, J. W., Wood, J. S., & Bradford, D. C. (1984). Aerobic exercise training and improved neuropsychological function of older individuals. *Neurobiology of Aging, 5,* 35–42.

Erber, J. T. (1981). Remote memory and age: A review. *Experimental Aging Research, 7,* 189–199.

Erikson, R. C., Poon, L. W., & Walsh-Sweeney, L. (1980). Clinical memory testing of the elderly. In L. W. Poon, J. L. Fozard, L. S. Cermak, D. Arenberg, & L. W. Thompson (Eds.), *New directions in memory and aging: Proceedings of the George A. Talland Memorial Conference.* Hillsdale, NJ: Lawrence Erlbaum Assoc.

Fozard, J. L., & Thomas, J. C. (1975). Psychology of aging: Basic findings and their psychiatric applications. In J. G. Howells (Ed.) *Modern perspectives in the psychiatry of old age.* NY: Brunner/Mazel.

Gholson, B. (1980). *The cognitive-developmental basis of human learning: Studies in hypothesis testing.* New York: Academic Press.

Gonda, J., Quayhagen, M., & Schaie, K. W. (1981). Education, task meaningfulness, and cognitive performance in young-old and old-old adults. *Educational Gerontology, 7,* 151–158.

Granick, S., & Friedman, A. S. (1973). Educational experience and maintenance of intellectual functioning by the aged: An overview. In L. F. Jarvik, C. Eisdorfer, & J. E. Blum (Eds.), *Intellectual functioning in adults.* New York: Springer.

Gruneberg, M. M., & Morris, P. E. (Eds.) (1979). *Applied problems in memory.* London: Academic Press.

Gruneberg, M. M., Morris, P. E., & Sykes, R. N. (Eds.) (1978). *Practical aspects of memory.* London: Academic Press.

Hanley-Dunn, P., & McIntosh, J. L. (1984). Meaningfulness and recall of names by young and old adults. *Journal of Gerontology, 39,* 583–585.

Harris, J. E. (1978). External memory aids. In M. M. Gruneberg, P. E.

Morris, & R. N. Sykes (Eds.), *Practical aspects of memory*. London: Academic Press.

Harris, J. E. (1980). Memory aids people use: Two interview studies. *Memory & Cognition, 8,* 31–38.

Harris, J. E. (1984). Remembering to do things: A forgotton topic. In J. E. Harris & P. E. Morris (Eds.), *Everyday memory, actions and absent-mindedness*. London: Academic Press.

Harris, J. E., & Morris, P. E. (Eds.) (1984). *Everyday memory, actions and absent-mindedness*. London: Academic Press.

Hasher, L., & Zacks, R. T. (1979). Automatic and effortful processes in memory. *Journal of Experimental Psychology: General, 108,* 356–388.

Hellebusch, S. J. (1976). On improving learning and memory in the aged: The effects of mnemonics on strategy, transfer, and generalization. Dissertation. University of Notre Dame.

Higbee, K. L. (1977). *Your memory: How it works and how to improve it.* Englewood Cliffs, NJ: Prentice-Hall.

Horn, J. L., & Cattell, R. B. (1967). Age differences in fluid and crystallized intelligence. *Acta Psychologia, 26,* 107–129.

Hoyer, W. J., & Plude, D. J. (1980). Attentional and perceptual processes in the study of cognitive aging. In L. W. Poon (Ed.), *Aging in the 1980s.* Washington, DC: American Psychological Association.

Hoyer, W. J., Raskind, C. L., & Abrahams, J. P. (1984). Research practices in the psychology of aging: A survey of research published in the Journal of Gerontology, 1975–1982. *Journal of Gerontology, 39,* 44–48.

Hulicka, I. M. (1967). Age differences in retention as a function of interference. *Journal of Gerontology, 22,* 180–184.

Hulicka, I. M. (1982). Memory functioning in late adulthood. In F. I. M. Craik & S. Trehub (Eds.), *Aging and cognitive processes*. New York: Plenum Press.

Hulicka, I. M., & Grossman, J. L. (1967). Age-group comparisons for the use of mediators in paired-associate learning. *Journal of Gerontology, 22,* 46–51.

Hulicka, I. M., & Weiss, R. (1965). Age differences in retention as a function of learning. *Journal of Counseling Psychology, 29,* 125–129.

Hultsch, D. F. (1969). Adult age differences in the organization of free recall. *Developmental Psychology, 1,* 673–678.

Hultsch, D. F., & Deutsch, F. (1981). *Adult development and aging.* New York: McGraw-Hill.

Hultsch, D. F., & Pentz, C. A. (1980). Encoding, storage, and retrieval in adult memory: The role of model assumptions. In L. W. Poon, J. L. Fozard, L. S. Cermak, D. Arenberg, & L. W. Thompson (Eds.), *New directions in memory and aging: Proceedings of the George A. Talland Memorial Conference.* Hillsdale, NJ: Lawrence Erlbaum Assoc.

Huyck, M. H., & Hoyer, W. J. (1982). *Adult development and aging.* Belmont, CA: Wadsworth.

Kail, R. (1979). *The development of memory in children.* San Francisco: W. H. Freeman.

Kausler, D. H. (1982). *Experimental psychology and human aging.* New York: John Wiley.

Kausler, D. H. (in press). Episodic memory: Memorizing performance. In N. Charness (Ed.), *Aging and human performance.* Chichester, England: John Wiley.

Kinsbourne, M. (1980). Attentional dysfunctions and the elderly: Theoretical models and research perspectives. In L. W. Poon, J. L. Fozard, L. S. Cermak, D. Arenberg, & L. W. Thompson (Eds.), *New directions in memory and aging: Proceedings of the George A. Talland Memorial Conference.* Hillsdale, NJ: Lawrence Erlbaum Assoc.

Kirasic, K. C., & Allen, G. L. (in press). Aging, spatial performance, and spatial competence. In N. Charness (Ed.), *Aging and human performance.* Chicester, England: John Wiley.

Lachman, M. E., & Jelalian, E. (1984). Self-efficacy and attributions for intellectual performance in young and elderly adults. *Journal of Gerontology, 39,* 577–582.

Lachman, J. L., & Lachman, R. (1980). Age and the actualization of world knowledge. In L. W. Poon, J. L. Fozard, L. S. Cermak, D. Arenberg, & L. W. Thompson (Eds.), *New directions in memory and aging: Proceedings of the George A. Talland Memorial Conference.* Hillsdale, NJ: Lawrence Erlbaum Assoc.

Lachman, R., Lachman, J. L., & Butterfield, E. C. (1979). *Cognitive psychology and information processing.* Hillsdale, NJ: Lawrence Erlbaum Assoc.

Lachman, R., Lachman, J. L., & Taylor, D. W. (1982). Reallocation of mental resources over the productive lifespan: Assumptions and task analyses. In F. I. M. Craik & S. Trehub (Eds.), *Aging and cognitive processes.* New York: Plenum Press.

Langer, E., & Avorn, J. (1982). Impact of the psychosocial environment of the elderly on behavioral and health outcomes. In R. Chellis & J. Seagle (Eds.), *Congregate housing for older people.* Lexington, MA: D. C. Heath.

Langer, E., & Rodin, J. (1976). The effects of enhanced personal responsibility for the aged: A field experiment in an institutional setting. *Journal of Personality and Social Psychology, 1976, 34,* 191–198.

Lawton, M. P., & Nahemow, L. (1973). Ecology and the aging process. In C. Eisdorfer & M. P. Lawton (Eds.), *The psychology of adult development and aging.* Washington, DC: American Psychological Association.

Loftus, E. F. (1975). Leading questions and the eyewitness report. *Cognitive Psychology, 7,* 560–577.

Loftus, E. F. (1979). *Eyewitness testimony.* Cambridge, MA: Harvard University Press.

Loftus, E. F. (1980). *Memory.* Reading, MA: Addison-Wesley.

Loftus, E. F., Miller, D. G., & Burns, H. J. (1978). Semantic integration of verbal information into a visual memory. *Journal of Experimental Psychology: Human Learning and Memory, 4,* 19–31.

Loftus, E. F., & Palmer, J. C. (1974). Reconstruction of automobile destruction: An example of the interaction between language and memory. *Journal of Verbal Learning and Verbal Behavior, 13,* 585–589.

Lorayne, H., & Lucas, J. (1974). *The Memory Book.* New York: Ballantine Books.

Lowenthal, M. F., Berkman, P. L., Buehler, J. A., Pierce, R. C., Robinson, B. C., & Trier, M. L. (1967). *Aging and mental disorder in San Francisco.* San Francisco: Jossey Bass.

Luria, A. R. (1968). *The mind of a mnemonist* (trans. Lynn Solotaroff). New York: Basic Books.

Mace, N. L. & Robins, P. V. (1981). *The 36-hour day.* Baltimore: The Johns Hopkins University Press.

McCarthy, M., Ferris, S. H., Clark, E., & Crook, T. (1981). Acquisition and retention of categorized material in normal aging and senile dementia. *Experimental Aging Research, 7,* 127–135.

Meichenbaum, D. (1974). Self-instructional training: A cognitive prosthesis for the aged. *Human Development, 17,* 273–280.

Miller, N. W., & Cohen, G. D. (Eds.) (1981). *Clinical aspects of Alzheimer's disease and senile dementia.* New York: Raven Press.

Mistler-Lachman, J. L. (1977). Spontaneous shift in encoding dimensions among elderly subjects. *Journal of Gerontology, 32,* 68–72.

Monge, R. H., & Hultsch, D. F. (1971). Paired-associate learning as a function of adult age and the length of the anticipation and inspection intervals. *Journal of Gerontology, 26,* 157–162.

Morris, C. D., Bransford, J. D., & Franks, J. J. (1977). Levels of processing versus transfer appropriate processing. *Journal of Verbal Learning and Verbal Behavior, 16,* 519–533.

Morris, P. E. (1979). Strategies for learning and recall. In M. M. Gruneberg & P. E. Morris (Eds.), *Applied problems in memory.* London: Academic Press.

Morris, P. E. (1984). The validity of subjective reports on memory. In J. E. Harris & P. E. Morris (Eds.), *Everyday memory, actions and absent-mindedness.* London: Academic Press.

Moscovitch, M. C. (1982). A neuropsychological approach to perception and memory in normal and pathological aging. In F. I. M. Craik & S. Trehub (Eds.), *Aging and cognitive processes.* New York: Plenum Press.

Murphy, M. D., Sanders, R. E., Gabriesheski, A. S., & Schmitt, F. A. (1981). Metamemory in the aged. *Journal of Gerontology, 36,* 185–193.

Murrell, H. (1970). The effect of extensive practice on age differences in reaction time. *Journal of Gerontology, 25,* 268–274.

Murrell, H., & Edwards, E. (1963). Field studies of an indicator machine tool travel with special reference to the ageing [sic] worker. *Occupational Psychology, 37,* 267–275.

Murrell, H., & Humphries, S. (1978). Age, experience, and short-term memory. In M. M. Gruneberg, P. E. Morris, & R. N. Sykes (Eds.), *Practical aspects of memory.* London: Academic Press.

Murrell, H., Powesland, P. F., & Forsaith, B. (1962). A study of pillar-drilling in relation to age. *Occupational Psychology, 36,* 45–52.

Neisser, U. (1982). *Memory observed.* San Francisco: W. H. Freeman

Nickerson, R. S. (1980). Retrieval efficiency, knowledge assessment and age: Comments on some welcome findings. In L. W. Poon, J. L. Fozard, L. S. Cermak, D. Arenberg, & L. W. Thompson (Eds.), *New directions in memory and aging: Proceedings of the George A. Talland Memorial Conference.* Hillsdale, NJ: Lawrence Erlbaum Assoc.

Pentz, C. A., III, Elias, M. F., Wood, W. G., Schultz, N. R., & Dineen, J. (1979). Relationship of age and hypertension to neuropsychological test performance. *Experimental Aging Research, 5,* 351–372.

Perlmuter, L. C. (1985, March). Motivation. Paper presented at the George A. Talland Memorial Conference, Boston.

Perlmutter, M. (1978). What is memory aging the aging of? *Developmental Psychology, 14,* 330–345.

Perlmutter, M., (1980). An apparent paradox about memory aging. In L. W. Poon, J. L. Fozard, L. S. Cermak, D. Arenberg, L. W. Thompson (Eds.), *New directions in memory and aging: Proceedings of the George A. Talland Memorial Conference.* Hillsdale, NJ: Lawrence Erlbaum Assoc.

Perlmutter, M. & Mitchell, D. B. (1982). The appearance and disappearance of age differences in adult memory. In F. I. M. Craik & S. Trehub (Eds.), *Aging and cognitive processes.* New York: Plenum Press.

Poon, L. W. (Ed.) (1980a). *Aging in the 1980s.* Washington, DC: American Psychological Association.

Poon, L. W. (1980b). A systems approach for the assessment and treatment of memory problems. In J. M. Ferguson & C. B. Taylor (Eds.), *The comprehensive handbook of behavioral medicine* (Vol. 1). New York: Spectrum.

Poon, L. W., & Fozard, J. L. (1978). Speed of retrieval from long-term memory in relation to age, familiarity and datedness of information. *Journal of Gerontology, 33,* 711–717.

Poon, L. W., & Fozard, J. L. (1980). Age and word frequency effects in continuous recognition memory. *Journal of Gerontology, 35,* 77–86.

Poon, L. W., Fozard, J. L., Cermak, L. S., Arenberg, D., & Thompson, L. W. (Eds.) (1980). *New directions in memory and aging: Proceedings of the George A. Talland Memorial Conference.* Hillsdale, NJ: Lawrence Erlbaum Assoc.

Poon, L. W., & Walsh-Sweeney, L. (1981). Effects of bizarre and interacting imagery on learning and retrieval of the aged. *Experimental Aging Research, 7,* 65–70.

Poon, L. W., Walsh-Sweeney, L., & Fozard, J. L. (1980). Memory skill training for the elderly: Salient issues on the use of imagery mnemonics. In L. W. Poon, J. L. Fozard, L. S. Cermak, D. Arenberg, & L. W. Thompson (Eds.), *New directions in memory and aging: Proceedings of the George A. Talland Memorial Conference.* Hillsdale, NJ: Lawrence Erlbaum Assoc.

Popkin, S. J., Gallagher, D., Thompson, L. W., & Moore, M. (1982). Memory complaint and performance in normal and depressed older adults. *Experimental Aging Research, 8,* 141–145.

Reason, J. T. (1977). Skill and error in everyday life. In M. J. A. Howe (Ed.), *Adult learning.* London: John Wiley.

Reason, J. T. (1979). Actions not as planned: The price of automatisation [sic] In G. Underwood and R. Stevens (Eds.), *Aspects of consciousness: Psychological issues* (Vol. 1). London: Academic Press.

Reason, J. T. (1982). Lapses of attention in everyday life. In R. Parasuraman & D. R. Davies (Eds.), *Varieties of attention.* Orlando: Academic Press.

Reason, J. (1984). Absent-mindedness and cognitive control. In J. E. Harris & P. E. Morris (Eds.), *Everyday memory, actions and absent-mindedness.* London: Academic Press.

Reason, J. T., and Mycielska, K. (1982). *Absent-minded? The psychology of mental lapses and everyday errors.* Englewood Cliffs, NJ: Prentice-Hall.

Rebok, G. W., & Offermann, L. R. (1983). Behavioral competencies of older college students: A self-efficacy approach. *The Gerontologist, 23,* 428-432.

Robertson-Tchabo, E. A., Hausman, C. P., & Arenberg, D. (1976). A classical mnemonic for older learners: A trip that works. *Educational Gerontology, 1,* 215-226.

Salthouse, T. A. (1980). Age and memory: Strategies for localizing the loss. In L. W. Poon, J. L. Fozard, L. S. Cermak, D. Arenberg, & L. W. Thompson (Eds.), *New directions in memory and aging: Proceedings of the George A. Talland Memorial Conference.* Hillsdale, NJ: Lawrence Erlbaum Assoc.

Salthouse, T. A. (1982). *Adult cognition.* NY: Springer-Verlag.

Schaie, K. W. (1978). External validity in the assessment of intellectual development in adulthood. *Journal of Gerontology, 33,* 695-701.

Schmitt, F. A., Murphy, M. D., & Sanders, R. E. (1981). Training older adult free recall rehearsal strategies. *Journal of Gerontology, 36,* 329-337.

Simon, E. (1979). Depth and elaboration of processing in relation to age. *Journal of Experimental Psychology: Human Learning and Memory, 5,* 115-124.

Smith, A. D. (1980). Age differences in encoding, storage, and retrieval. In L. W. Poon, J. L. Fozard, L. S. Cermak, D. Arenberg, & L. W. Thompson (Eds.), *New directions in memory and aging: Proceedings of the George A. Talland Memorial Conference.* Hillsdale, NJ: Lawrence Erlbaum Assoc.

Smith, J., Heckhausen, J., Kliegl, R., & Baltes, P. B. (1984, November). Cognitive reserve capacity, expertise, and aging: Plasticity of digit span performance. Paper presented at the meeting of the Gerontological Society of America, San Antonio.

Spieth, W. (1965). Slowness of task performance and cardiovascular diseases. In A. T. Welford & J. E. Birren (Eds.), *Behavior, aging, and the nervous system.* Springfield, IL: Charles C. Thomas.

Sternberg, S. (1970). Memory scanning: Mental processes revealed by reaction-time experiments. In J. S. Antrobus (Ed.), *Cognition and affect.* Boston: Little, Brown.

Storandt, M., Grant, E. A., & Gordon, B. C. (1978). Remote memory as a function of age and sex. *Experimental Aging Research, 4,* 365-375.

Storandt, M., Siegler, I. C., & Elias, M. F. (Eds.) (1978). *The clinical psychology of aging.* New York: Plenum Press.

Thomas, J. C., Waugh, N. C., & Fozard, J. L. (1978). Age and familiarity in memory scanning. *Journal of Gerontology, 33,* 528–533.

Treat, N. J., Poon, L. W., & Fozard, J. L. (1981). Age, imagery, and practice in paired-associate learning. *Experimental Aging Research, 7,* 337–342.

Treat, N. J., Poon, L. W., Fozard, J. L., & Popkin, S. J. (1978). Toward applying cognitive skill training to memory problems. *Experimental Aging Research, 4,* 305–319.

Tulving, E., & Thomson, D. M. (1973). Encoding specificity and retrieval processes in episodic memory. *Psychological Review, 80,* 352–373.

Waugh, N. C., & Barr, R. A. (1980). Memory and mental tempo. In L. W. Poon, J. L. Fozard, L. S. Cermak, D. Arenberg, & L. W. Thompson (Eds.), *New directions in memory and aging: Proceedings of the George A. Talland Memorial Conference.* Hillsdale, NJ: Lawrence Erlbaum Assoc.

Welford, A. T. (1984). Between bodily changes and performance: Some possible reasons for slowing with age. *Experimental Aging Research, 10,* 73–88.

West, R. L. (1984, August). Analysis of prospective everyday memory. Paper presented at the meeting of the American Psychological Association, Toronto.

West, R. L. (1985, March). Practical mnemonics for the aged. Paper presented at the George A. Talland Memorial Conference. Boston.

West, R. L., & Boatwright, L. K. (1983). Adult age differences in cued recall and recognition under varying encoding and retrieval conditions. *Experimental Aging Research, 9,* 185–189.

West, R. L., Boatwright, L. K., & Schleser, R. (1984). The link between memory performance, self-assessment, and affective status. *Experimental Aging Research, 10,* 197–200.

West, R. L., & Cohen, S. (1985). The systematic use of semantic and acoustic processing by younger and older adults. *Experimental Aging Research, 11,* 81–86.

West, R. L., & Walton, M. (1985, March). Practical memory functioning in the elderly. Paper presented at the National Forum on Research in Aging, Lincoln, NE.

Wilkins, A. J., & Baddeley, A. (1978). Remembering to recall in everyday life: An approach to absent-mindedness. In M. M. Gruneberg, P. E. Morris, & R. N. Sykes (Eds.), *Practical aspects of memory.* London: Academic Press.

Willis, S. L., & Baltes, P. B. (1980). Intelligence in adulthood and aging: Contemporary issues. In L. W. Poon (Ed.), *Aging in the 1980s.* Washington, DC: American Psychological Association.

Wilson, B. A., & Moffat, N. (1984). *Clinical management of memory problems.* Rockville, MD: Aspen.

Winocur, G. (1982). Learning and memory deficits in institutionalized and noninstitutionalized old people: An analysis of interference effects. In

F. I. M. Craik, & S. Trehub (Eds.), *Aging and cognitive processes*. New York: Plenum Press.

Yesavage, J. (1983). Imagery pretraining and memory training in the elderly. *International Journal of Experimental and Clinical Gerontology, 29,* 271–275.

Yesavage, J. A. (1985, March). Mnemonics as modifed for use by the elderly. Paper presented at the George A. Talland Memorial Conference, Boston.

Yesavage, J. A., Rose, T. L., & Spiegel, D. (1982). Relaxation training and memory improvement in elderly normals: Correlation of anxiety ratings and recall improvement. *Experimental Aging Research, 8,* 195–198.

Zarit, S. H., Cole, K. D., & Guider, R. L. (1981). Memory training strategies and subjective complaints of memory in the aged. *The Gerontologist, 21,* 158–164.

Zarit, S. H., Gallagher, D., & Kramer, N. (1981). Memory training in the community aged: Effects on depression, memory complaint, and memory performance. *Educational Gerontology, 6,* 11–27.

Zechmeister, E. B., & Nyberg, S. E. (1982). *Human memory*. Belmont, CA: Wadsworth.

Zelinski, E. M., Gilewski, M. J., & Thompson, L. W. (1980). Do laboratory tests relate to self-assessment of memory ability in the young and old? In L. W. Poon, J. L. Fozard, L. S. Cermak, D. Arenberg, & L. W. Thompson (Eds.), *New directions in memory and aging: Proceedings of the George A. Talland Memorial Conference*. Hillsdale, NJ: Lawrence Erlbaum Assoc.

Index